W0247899

Abschlussprüfung

Englisch

Lösungsheft

Realschule
Baden-Württemberg

Cornelsen

Lösungen zu den Aufgaben innerhalb der Lerntipps *page 4–11*

'working as an au pair' (Lösungsvorschlag – andere Lösungen sind möglich): *page 5*

1. Do you think I'm old enough to work as an au pair?
2. Are there enough jobs?
3. Where did you work?
4. How big was your family?
5. Did you have enough free time?

'Please fill in the correct forms of the verb ...' *page 6*

1. goes
2. met
3. hadn't seen
4. asked
5. has phoned
6. hasn't given
7. is waiting
8. will be

'Read the text. Find suitable forms of the words ...' *page 6*

1. ask
2. going
3. extremely
4. don't like
5. have had to / have to
6. watching
7. hard
8. do
9. easily
10. properly

Formal letter *page 6*

Dear Sir or Madam,
I am writing about a computer that I bought from your company. I have had a lot of problems with it, and when I phoned your hotline, I did not get any help.
I am very unhappy with this situation and I think your company should help me more.
I look forward to hearing from you.
Yours faithfully
Mandy Hill

common mistakes *page 8*

1. There are ...
2. ... for many years
3. ... taller than ...
4. ... needn't hurry ...
5. ... often go ...
6. Most kids ...
7. ... worked hard ...
8. Do you sometimes do ...
9. ... plays ... well
10. ... is ringing
11. This information is ...
12. ... a nurse
13. ... often plays ...
14. ... by a dog, ...
15. ... played ...
16. She enjoys speaking ...
17. We've been here ...
18. ... people who ...

translation exercise *page 9*

1. Ihr Bruder kam gestern kurz vor Mitternacht nach Hause.
2. Sie fahren gerne Ski.
3. Ich schaute mir das Spiel im Fernsehen an.
4. Sie brauchte fünf Minuten, um dort hinzukommen.
5. Wir machen das später.

1 Global Pizza

A. Text-based Tasks *page 13*

1
1. false
2. true
3. false
4. true

2
1. It is easy to make, easy to serve and more varied than the hamburger.
2. The Greeks ate 'plakuntos' and the Romans ate 'picea'.
3. It was the pizza capital of the world.

3 *Possible questions:*
What was the food like? / Was the food good?
Were you sometimes still hungry after a meal?
What did you have for breakfast?
Could you eat as much as you wanted?
What kind of things did you eat?

B. Use of Language *page 14*

1
1. delivery
2. tiring
3. careful
4. slippery
5. dangerous
6. friendly
7. annoying
8. angrily
9. best
10. learning
11. have discovered
12. I'm starving

2 *Possible questions:*
1. This means that something can be found all over the world.
2. This is the name given to the ingredients you put on a pizza base (ham, cheese, tomato, etc).
3. A century is a period of 100 years.
4. The capital of a product is the place which is most famous for it.

3
1. gradually (line 7)
2. various (line 11)
3. similar (line 13)

C. Creative Writing *page 15*

1 1. I would first ask the other passengers if it belongs to anyone or if they had seen the person sitting there. Then I would go to the front of the bus and tell the driver. He would probably call the appropriate office at the bus station to take a closer look at the backpack. *(54 words)*

3. I would tell my mother that it wasn't my fault and that it was not fair to stop me from seeing my friends. I would promise not to come home late again and try and persuade her to change her mind. If she still didn't agree, I would feel very cross and go up to my room. *(57 words)*

2 A The origin of umbrella hats
A friend of my father's invented umbrella hats. He got the idea when he went out running near his house one day. He was wearing a cap because it was hot and sunny. But the sky became grey and it started to rain. He turned round and started to run home quickly but it rained harder and harder and he got very wet. So when he got home, he took his little daughter's toy umbrella and fixed it to a metal headband. He put it on his head and opened the umbrella. It was perfect! When his friends saw it, they wanted one, too, so he made one for all of them. And now the umbrella hat is famous everywhere. (125 words)

B Hi Mike! You asked me about that new fast food restaurant near our school. You can get burgers and chips and also hotdogs and pizzas. They sell soft drinks, too. It is not very expensive and it is as good as the other fast food places in town. I don't like the tables and chairs much because they are bright red and yellow but the people who work there are very friendly. They know us quite well now because we often go there instead of staying in the canteen at school, especially when a class is cancelled after lunch. It gives us a long lunch-hour. There is a jukebox there and we listen to music, but the best thing is the TV on the wall which has all the sports channels. *(125 words)*

D. Skills and Techniques *page 16–17*

1
1. Ursprünglich kamen Hamburger und Hot Dogs aus Deutschland, Pasta and Spaghetti aus Italien und das Sandwich aus England.
2. Beide Gerichte kamen durch Einwanderer aus Deutschland in die USA.
3. Im Brötchen sind sie einfacher zu essen.
4. Sandwich ist eine Stadt im Süden Englands.
5. Nein. (Die Italiener machen diese Gerichte seit Jahrhunderten.)
6. Es gibt Hunderte von Pastaformen.
7. Pasta wird aus Mehl und Wasser gemacht.

2 Die Pizza ist mit den Italienern zum Ende des 19. Jahrhunderts in die USA eingewandert. Die erste Pizzeria in den Vereinigten Staaten wurde 1905 von Gennaro Lombardi in der Spring Street 53½ in New York eröffnet. Doch die Beliebtheit der Pizza steigerte sich rasant, als amerikanische Soldaten nach dem 2. Weltkrieg aus Italien heimkehrten und von diesem „phantastischen italienischen Gericht" schwärmten. Heutzutage sind die Amerikaner die größten Hersteller und Verbraucher der Pizza weltweit.

2 The Clown Doctor

A. Text-based Tasks page 19

1 *Possible answers:*
1. she was eight years old.
2. they wouldn't be able to cheer up sick children / children wouldn't laugh / they'd be useless.
3. Lucy (and her colleague) meet the nurses and doctors.
4. distracts them so that the nurses can do their job.

2 *Individual answers:*
1. She is hard-working, caring and probably a very strong person.
2. They feel happy and, therefore, they feel much better.
3. They participate in events to raise money for the Theodora Children's Trust.

3 *Possible questions:*
Do you enjoy your work?
Are you sad when you see the sick children?
How many children do you see at the hospital?
How often do you go to the hospital?
Is it difficult to learn to be a clown doctor?

B. Use of Language page 20

1 This means:
1. ... make your face look funny so that people laugh at you.
2. ... take another person's hand when you say 'hello' or 'good-bye'.
3. ... make ill children feel happier.
4. ... become good friends with someone.

2
1. left
2. had taught (had been teaching)
3. fascinated
4. description
5. poverty
6. interested
7. easily
8. wrote
9. replacement
10. beginning
11. heat
12. feeling
13. exciting

C. Creative Writing *page 21*

1 The Theodora Children's Trust is looking for an experienced clown to be a clown doctor.
A clown doctor:
– visits sick children in hospital and entertains them.
– must be funny and inventive and make children laugh.
– should understand sick children's problems and how they feel.
– must work with the nurses and doctors.
Please write to ... *(54 words)*

2 A Today two clowns came to the hospital. They made funny faces, told jokes and did magic tricks. One of them was called Doctor LooLoo. When she walked into the ward, she was blowing bubbles. She was wearing a fancy coat, a yellow shirt and striped tights. Her hair was in plaits and she had a red rubber nose. She came over to me and shook my hand. The two clowns told us some funny stories and sang some nonsense songs. They also made some balloon animals out of some special balloons they had brought with them.
It was a lot of fun. They really cheered me up and I forgot that I was sick! They are coming back next week and I am already looking forward to it. *(128 words)*

B The Theodora Children's Trust sends clowns into hospital to cheer up sick children. They are called clown doctors but they are not medical doctors. They visit the children and make them laugh. Many of the children are very ill. They often spend a long time in hospital and this makes them sad and depressed. When the clown doctors come and see them, the children laugh at their funny games and tricks and this makes them feel better. The doctors and nurses often ask the clown doctors to be withthe children when they have to have an injection or take horrible medicine. Clown doctors do an important job and The Theodora Trust needs money to send more of them into hospitals. *(121 words)*

D. Skills and Techniques *page 22–23*

1 What exactly does the Theodora Children's Trust do?
Der Theodora Children's Trust ist eine Organisation, die Clown Doctors ausbildet und sie dann zu den einzelnen Krankenhäusern schickt, um dort kranke Kinder aufzumuntern.
How long has it existed?
Schon über zehn Jahre. Die ersten Clowns gingen bereits 1994 in ein großes Londoner Kinderkrankenhaus.
What do clown doctors learn during their training?
Die Clown Doctors bekommen eine medizinische Ausbildung und lernen den Umgang mit kranken Kindern. In ihrer künstlerischen Ausbildung lernen sie zudem viele Mittel, um Kinder zu unterhalten.
How many hospitals in Great Britain work with clown doctors?
Gegenwärtig arbeiten Clown Doctors an etwa 10 großen britischen Krankenhäusern.

2 Clown in einem Krankenhaus zu sein ist sehr ermüdend, körperlich wie auch emotional. Wir müssen lernen, unsere Gefühle nicht zu zeigen, andernfalls wären wir nutzlos. Clown doctors sind empfindsam, aber diese Seite von ihnen wird von den meisten Menschen nicht wahrgenommen. Den Kindern gegenüber sind wir immerzu fröhlich. Ich lerne immer noch, mir selbst zuzugestehen, dass ich ab und zu traurig bin. Derzeit arbeite ich mit einem sehr kranken Mädchen aus Bosnien, das kein Englisch spricht, weshalb das Lachen unsere gemeinsame Sprache ist.

3 Surfing with Sharks

A. Text-based Tasks *page 25*

1
1. true
2. true
3. true
4. false

2
1. There are 390 species of shark.
2. The International Shark Attack File helps surfers and swimmers.
3. You should stay calm and leave the water quickly and quietly.

3 *Possible questions:*

Did you see the shark before it attacked you?
What did the shark do to you?
How did you get out of the water?
Do you still go surfing?
Are you frightened?
What is the film about the incident called?

B. Use of Language *page 26*

1
1. difference
2. scientists
3. automatically
4. specially
5. marked
6. feeling
7. keeper(s)
8. sleepy
9. worried
10. herself
11. had saved
12. boiling

2
1. If you are fond of something, you like it or enjoy it.
2. A marine biologist is a scientist who studies plants and animals in the sea.
3. These are the techniques fishermen use to catch fish.
4. This is a box or a bag of basic medical necessities like a bandage, plasters, antiseptic cream, etc.

3
1. below (line 12)
2. hard (line 18)
3. growing (line 40)

C. Creative Writing *page 27*

1
1. If the person was in the water quite near the beach, I would try and pull him or her out. But if the person was a long way from the beach, I would run as fast as I could to the nearest person on the beach and ask for help. I would ask them to phone the lifeguards or the police. *(61 words)*
3. I would go to see my friend who lives next door. I would explain the problem and ask if I could stay in his house until one of my family members came back. I would watch TV or play on the computer. If my friend was not at home, I would sit on the ground by the door and wait! *(60 words)*

2

A Today I had my first windsurfing lesson. It is not as easy as it looks. First you have to push the board into deep water and then climb onto it. Then you stand up on the board – that was when I first fell off into the water! It took me some time to get my balance. When I finally managed and was able to pull up the sail, I started moving. It was a wonderful feeling – for as long as it lasted before I fell off into the water again! But with a little practice, I learned how to stand properly on the board and finally spent more time on the board than off it. I really enjoyed it and am looking forward to my second lesson tomorrow. *(128 words)*

B I was walking to my friend's house the other day when I saw a wallet on the pavement. I picked it up and opened it. There were some credit cards with the name 'Winston', some five-pound notes and a photo of a little boy in front of a house. Fortunately, I recognized the house, so I didn't have to search for the address. I went there and rang the bell. A lady opened the door. 'Are you Mrs Winston?', I asked her. 'Yes, I am,' she replied. I showed her the wallet. She was very surprised and looked inside it. Then she thanked me and put a note in my hand as a reward. I looked down. Ten pounds! More than a month's pocket money! *(126 words)*

D. Skills and Techniques *page 28–29*

1
1. Eine Küste und hohe Wellen.
2. Südafrika, Australien, Kalifornien, Indonesien, Frankreich
3. Hawaii liegt im Pazifik.
4. Auf Hawaii war Wellenreiten schon vor Jahrhunderten der traditionelle Zeitvertreib der örtlichen Fischer.
5. Nein. Nur eine Elite durfte entlang der besten Küsten surfen.
6. 1778 hat Captain Cook Hawaii entdeckt.
7. Er hat gesehen, wie die Einheimischen gesurft haben
8. Hawaii wurde zum neuesten Staat der Vereinigten Staaten.
9. Die amerikanische Lebensart hat Fuß gefasst.
10. Gäste bekommen Kränze aus Blumen oder Muscheln.

2 Wenn die Surfer auf das Meer hinausschwimmen und nach einer großen Welle Ausschau halten, dann bewegen sie dabei das Brett mit Armen und Beinen über das Wasser. Von unten gesehen, also von dort, wo die Haie sind, sehen die Surfer und ihre Bretter dann ähnlich aus wie Robben oder Schildkröten. Haie können nicht besonders gut sehen, daher greifen sie Surfer vermutlich nur aus Versehen an. Tatsächlich versuchen die Haie so gut wie nie, einen Surfer zu verspeisen, sobald sie merken, dass er oder sie nicht ihrer Lieblingsnahrung entspricht.

4 Earth Day

A. Text-based Tasks *page 31*

1
1. C
2. A
3. D
4. B
5. E

2
1. The idea of Earth Day is to celebrate the Earth and protest against pollution.
2. He saw pollution by rubbish and chemicals, dying forests and cities full of smog and car exhaust.
3. They help people plan demonstrations, campaigns, talks, and other activities.
4. They can organize clean-up campaigns, pick up rubbish or write letters to their local council.

3 *Possible questions:*
Why are you marching?
Are there many people there?
Are you carrying a banner?
What is written on it?
Where are you marching to?
Do you think this will help the environment?

B. Use of Language *page 32*

1
1. wildest
2. particularly
3. peaceful
4. relaxing
5. impressive
6. exciting
7. rocky
8. useful
9. lost
10. traditional
11. comfortable
12. setting off

2
1. This is when people come together for a special occasion like a birthday or anniversary.
2. This means everything that people throw away.
3. This means the world around us.

3
1. purpose (line 3)
2. throughout (line 29)
3. participate (line 43)

C. CREATIVE WRITING page 33

1 1. I would follow the girl out of the shop and talk to her. I would tell her she shouldn't have done that and try and persuade her not to do it again. I would explain that stealing even small things was not fair on the shopkeeper. I would ask her how she would feel if someone stole something from her. *(60 words)*

3. First of all I would go down to the beach and look at the oil. Then I would ask if I could help to clean up the beach. I would ask some friends to come with me. I would put on my boots and my raincoat and spend the day on the beach rescuing birds and scraping oil off the rocks. *(61 words)*

2 A Last week I went round the whole school from the top to the ground floor. In all the corridors, the lower part of the walls are cracked and dirty where pupils have kicked them. A lot of the desk tops in the classrooms have been damaged by sharp objects. In the toilets, there is graffiti on the doors and walls. In the playground, although there are plenty of rubbish bins, there are empty packets of biscuits and paper bags on the ground. I saw old scarves and gloves in the branches of the trees and the basketball posts have been bent and damaged. And I found a maths and a geography book lying in the rain! Who do they belong to? *(121 words)*

B The noise got louder and louder. So I got up and went over to the window, opened the curtains and looked out. I saw the strangest thing. It was a big old-fashioned lorry with glass sides. And through the glass I could see two lions walking up and down in the small space, looking out into the road. On the top of the lorry was a big notice saying 'Barnum's Circus is coming to your town. Don't miss it!'. The loudspeaker was playing loud music and the man next to the driver was speaking into a microphone at the same time. It was a terrible noise and nobody could hear a word he was saying! *(120 words)*

D. SKILLS AND TECHNIQUES page 34–35

1 1. Man kann schon Einfluss nehmen, indem man über die Umweltproblematik spricht und darüber hinaus versucht, sich selbst möglichst umweltfreundlich zu verhalten..

2. Anstatt sich mit dem Auto fahren zu lassen, kann man genauso gut zu Fuß gehen oder mit dem Fahrrad fahren. Man kann car-sharing organisieren, das heißt sein eigenes Auto in Nutzergemeinschaften mit anderen teilen. Schließlich kann man seine Eltern durchaus dazu anhalten, sämtliche Besorgungen auf einmal zu erledigen, sodass mehrere Autofahrten entfallen.

3. Die Herstellung von Plastiktüten ist sehr umweltbelastend und es dauert viele Jahre, bis sie natürlich abgebaut werden.

4. Es ist ganz einfach: Es genügt, die Produktbeschreibungen genau zu lesen und möglichst Produkte mit hohen chemischen Anteilen zu meiden.

5. Weil wir schlicht Teil dieser Natur sind. Das Gleichgewicht der Natur zu stören heißt unsere eigene Umwelt zu gefährden.

2 Stell dir einen Tag vor, an dem 500 Millionen Menschen aus 184 Ländern der ganzen Welt zusammenkommen, um für einen einzigen Zweck zu feiern und zu protestieren. Genau das ist am 22. April 2000 geschehen. An diesem Tag war ‚Earth Day' und der Zweck, den diese Leute im Sinn hatten, war, etwas für eine gesündere und sicherere Welt für jeden Einzelnen zu tun. Es war die größte Veranstaltung dieser Art in der Geschichte der Menschheit.

5 Sailing Teens

A. Text-based Tasks *page 37*

1
1. (He is) a sailing instructor.
2. (Seb spent) every free moment training for the race.
3. The boats were identical.
4. (They sailed) from Tenerife, Spain to Antigua.
5. Seb's dad won the race.

2
1. Ben
2. Seb
3. Giorgina
4. Catherine
5. Ben
6. Giorgina

3 *Possible questions:*
How long did it take you?
What was the weather like?
Did you have any storms?
How did you manage to sleep?
What did you eat?
Were you afraid?
Were you lonely?
Could you see your father's boat?
Would you like to do it again?

B. Use of Language *page 38*

1
1. professional
2. emigration
3. brought
4. disappearance
5. left
6. Hopeful
7. possibility
8. poverty
9. understandable
10. unbelievable
11. amazing
12. fame
13. exaggeration
14. national

2
1. set sail (line 12)
2. aboard (line 15)
3. a solo voyage (line 20)
4. to express your thoughts (line 36)
5. the chance (line 41)
6. no wonder (line 52)

C. Creative Writing *page 39*

1 1. I agree that sailing is a sport for rich people. It isn't a simple sport where you just need your hands and feet and a ball. You need a boat. And boats are very expensive to buy. And when you are not sailing in your boat, it costs a lot to rent a space to keep it in the harbour. *(60 words)*

2. I think sailing is one of the most exciting and interesting sports. It is a sport where there is a lot of variety and you have to be good at doing many things. You need to be physically fit because there is a lot of climbing and pulling to do. Also, you have to know how to use all the technical equipment on board. *(60 words)*

2 A Hi Frank
I have just come back from a holiday club. I had a really good time. I was in a room with three others andwe had a lot of fun. During the day there were lots of things to do. We went sailing and I learnt to water-ski! It's not easy! We also went hang-gliding – it is fantastic but I was a bit nervous at first! The food was quite good. We had a picnic at midday and a barbecue in the evening. We had to help with the washing-up afterwards! I played ping pong a lot and in the evening we played board games. We had a great party on the last evening!
Hope you had a good holiday, too. *(122 words)*

B Last year on holiday, some friends invited us to go sailing with them on their yacht but my sister wasn't well so we couldn't go. Our friends went off by themselves for the day. It was very hot and in the afternoon the sky became very dark and there was a terrible storm. The thunder roared and the lightning flashed. We thought about our friends at sea and hoped they had come back. The next day we didn't see them and we couldn't see their boat in the port. We were worried. We saw them three days later and learnt that they had been rescued by the lifeboat and had spent two days in hospital. Thank goodness we hadn't gone with them! *(122 words)*

D. Skills and Techniques *page 40–41*

1 1. Im Jahre 2004 gewann Ellen MacArthur das berühmte Vendée-Globe Rennen. Sie war die schnellste Seglerin der Welt und die jüngste Britin, die nonstop um die Welt gesegelt ist.
2. Ellen ist in Zentralengland, weit ab von der Küste, aufgewachsen.
3. Als sie acht Jahre alt war, nahm ihre Tante sie auf einen Segeltörn mit. Von diesem Augenblick an war sie für den Sport begeistert.
4. Drei Jahre lang hatte sie ihr Taschengeld gespart und ihre Großmutter legte noch etwas dazu.
5. Während des Vendée-Globe-Rennens war Ellen vollkommen auf sich selbst gestellt. Sie musste selbstständig Reparaturen durchführen, Seestürme bewältigen und Eisberge umschiffen. Zudem musste sie gegen ihre Erschöpfung ankämpfen und dabei ständig Kurs halten.
6. Mit 18 Jahren gewann Ellen den Young Sailor of the Year Award. Danach gewann sie den Titel Yachtsman of the Year. Schließlich gewann sie, 25-jährig, das Vendée-Globe-Rennen.
7. Ellen nimmt Kinder, die an Krebserkrankungen leiden, zu Segeltouren mit. Ein Foto von einem dieser Kinder – es ist das Bild eines lächelnden Mädchens – begleitet sie auf ihren Reisen.

2 „Ihr seid beide so ehrgeizig. Warum macht ihr nicht ein Rennen, um herauszufinden, wer der bessere Segler ist?" Seine Mutter machte nur Spaß, aber Seb und sein Vater nahmen die Idee durchaus ernst. Während der folgenden drei Jahre trainierte Seb jede freie Minute mit seinem Vater und am 19. Dezember 2002 setzte Seb in Teneriffa, Spanien, die Segel zum größten Abenteuer seines Lebens: einem Rennen gegen seinen Vater über den Atlantik.

6 One Who Understands

A. Text-based Tasks page 43

1
1. he didn't fit in with other kids.
2. he went to university.
3. young, multiracial people.
4. other people of mixed race and their experiences.
5. gives support to multiracial teens and their families.

2
1. At Matt's school there were white, black, Asian and Hispanic kids.
2. Matt has a Korean mother and a white father.
3. They are encouraged to write their own stories about being multiracial.

3 *Possible questions:*
How many pupils of mixed racial backgrounds are there at your school?
What kind of activities do you like doing in your leisure time?
Do you fit in with the other pupils who are not multiracial?
What are the main problems which are related to being multiracial?
What is your attitude concerning professional life after leaving school?

B. Use of Language page 44

1
1. really
2. depressing
3. danger
4. violence
5. vandalism
6. pollution
7. destruction
8. unhealthy
9. playing
10. unemployed
11. has shown
12. impression
13. freedom
14. activities

2
1. teenagers (line 4)
2. confused (line 16)
3. he realized (line 22)
4. he founded (line 25)
5. dated (line 34)
6. celebrities (line 36)

C. Creative Writing *page 45*

1
1. I would explain to the ticket seller that I had forgotten my card and I would ask him or her to let me have the reduction. I would tell him how old I was and which school I went to. If the person refused, I wouldn't buy a normal ticket. I would come back to see the film another time. *(60 words)*
2. I would go up to her during the break and ask her if she wanted some help. I would try to explain in simple words and sign language. I would try to be friends with her and ask the teacher if I could sit next to or near her in class so that I could explain things she didn't understand. *(60 words)*

2
A We have a new boy in class called James. He is from Edinburgh in Scotland and he speaks with a strong Scottish accent. Last week, James brought his father's kilt to school for World Day. This is a short tartan skirt that Scottish men often wear on special occasions. James asked me if I wanted to try it on, so I took off my jeans and put on the kilt. Then I stood on the desk and tried to do a Scottish dance. Everyone laughed. Just then the head teacher walked in. I was so embarrassed. She looked at me and then said, "Are you going to play us the bagpipes? If not, you'd better take off your kilt and sit down!" *(122 words)*

B Dear Gary
We had World Day at school last week. This is a day when each class organizes an activity based on different traditions in countries all over the world. Our class cooked food from Asian countries. We made some Japanese sushi – that is raw fish and rice, Chinese chop suey and spicy chicken from Thailand. Another class played South American Indian music with reed pipes and small drums. They wore brightly coloured clothes from Peru and Mexico. Form 5 dressed up in clothes from India and Africa. The girls wore Indian saris and the boys wore long cotton tunics. Other classes presented food from the Middle East and music from places in the West Indies, like Jamaica.
Does your school have World Day? Write and tell me, please. *(125 words)*

D. Skills and Techniques *page 46–47*

1
1. Das bedeutet eine Mischung von Menschen mit diverser Herkunft, Kultur, Religion und diversen Sprachen und Traditionen.
2. Die Weißen (75,1%) sind die größte ethnische Gruppe, die Native Americans (0,9%) die kleinste.
3. Die englische Sprache.
4. Indien, Pakistan, die Karibik
5. Man lernt andere Kulturen, Traditionen und Essen kennen. Es gibt mehr Möglichkeiten Fremdsprachen zu lernen. Man lernt, offener und toleranter zu sein.
6. Diese Kinder lernen offen zu sein und andere Kulturen und Sprachen leicht zu akzeptieren.
7. Diese Kinder haben manchmal Probleme mit der eigenen Identität. Manche können sich weder mit dem Herkunftsland der Mutter noch mit dem des Vaters identifizieren
8. Mit der Globalisierung ziehen immer mehr Menschen in andere Länder um und immer mehr Mischehen werden geschlossen.

2 Als Matt Kaley in den Vereinigten Staaten aufwuchs, stellte er sich oft die Frage: „Wer bin ich eigentlich?" Daran ist natürlich nichts Ungewöhnliches; die meisten Teenager stellen sich von Zeit zu Zeit genau diese Frage. Doch Matts Problem war ein ganz besonderes. Wenn er seine Mitschüler betrachtete, konnte er keinen finden, der so aussah wie er. Es gab weiße und schwarze, asiatische und Hispanic kids, aber keines sah so aus wie er.

7 Australian Connection

A. Text-based Tasks *page 49*

1
2. walk drive
3. all afternoon two hours
4. top foot
5. seven a couple of (OR two)
6. through the rain forest along the beach
7. along the beach through the rain forest
8. read about seen on television
9. down to the top of
10. the evening midday
11. shallow full (OR deep)
12. full shallow
13. only just managed to drive across drove across easily

2
1. City people buy the land because they want to build holiday homes.
2. There should be strict laws that prevent them from doing this.
3. The forests will slowly be destroyed.
4. I think they are very, very stupid.

3 *Possible questions:*
Where have you been and what have you done?
What's the rain forest like?
Are you and your father getting on well?
Are you enjoying being with him?

B. Use of Language *page 50–51*

1
1. fantastic (line 15) OR wonderful (line 16)
2. love (line 17)
3. angrily (line 38)
4. improved (line 40)
5. to cheer up (line 40)

2
1. imagination
2. explorers
3. length
4. variety
5. memorable
6. friendly
7. playful
8. brightly
9. sandy
10. ensure
11. tourists

3
1. across
2. out of
3. through
4. along
5. over
6. onto

C. Creative Writing *page 52*

1 You should take a backpack with a bottle of water and a pair of sunglasses. It is also useful to take some binoculars. You should wear shorts and a T-shirt, and walking shoes with cotton socks. You can take your shoes off and tie them round your neck when walking through water. Don't forget to wear a cap or a sunhat. *(61 words)*

2 A Hi Jack,
Thanks for your email. I am looking forward to the trip, too. You asked what we should do. Well, I have learned a lot about Australia in my geography lessons at school and I know it is a very big country and there is a lot to see.
One thing I really must visit is the Great Barrier Reef. I have seen pictures of it and would like to see the coral for myself.
Another thing I would like to do is to visit the rain forest. I would like to see some of the plants, animals and insects that I have only ever seen in pictures and films.
And, of course, a trip to the beach would be great.
Best wishes
Tom *(124 words)*

B Dear Dad
Thank you for a great holiday in Australia. I shall never forget the fantastic things we did.
I loved the trip to the rain forest and learning all about it. It was fun to see the crocodiles in the reserve, too. The most exciting part of the holiday was sailing out to the Great Barrier Reef. Do you remember those amazing dolphins swimming along with the boat? I took some really good photos of them. I'll send them to you. I have put my shells and pieces of coral on the shelf in my room. Thanks again for giving me such a good time. I really enjoyed being with you. Good luck with the 'Save the Rain Forest' campaign!
Write to me soon. *(125 words)*

D. Skills and Techniques *page 53–54*

1
1. Die Pflanzen wandeln Kohledioxyde in frische Luft um und verhindern den Treibhaus-Effekt.
2. 60% aller Medikamente gegen Krebs und andere lebensgefährliche Krankheiten werden aus Pflanzen gewonnen, die nur im Regenwald zu finden sind.
3. Eine trockene Wüste könnte entstehen.
4. Farmer und reiche Holz- bzw. Ölkonzerne.
5. Farmer räumen große Waldgebiete für die Rinderzucht. Das Fleisch wird an Hamburger Firmen verkauft.
6. Die Regenwälder sind überwiegend öffentliches Land.
7. Die Menschen werden von den Großkonzernen weggejagt.
8. Sie verlangen, dass der Raubbau aufhört. Das kann nur geschehen, wenn es entsprechende Gesetze gibt, die den Regenwald und die dort lebenden Menschen schützen.

2 Translation
Als sie den Regenwald hinter sich gelassen hatten und die Straßen besser wurden, besserte sich Toms Stimmung. Er erzählte Alex alles über das Boot, das er mit seinem Bruder teilte.

„Ich dachte, wir könnten sie zum Riff rausbringen", sagte er.
„Zum Great Barrier Riff?", fragte Alex ganz aufgeregt.
„Genau das meine ich", lachte Tom.
Alex grinste. Natürlich wusste er alles über das Great Barrier Riff. Er hatte davon schon im Geografieunterricht gehört und wollte immer einmal das farbenprächtige Riff mit eigenen Augen sehen. Genau das würde er jetzt tun.
„Ist es denn so wunderbar, wie es im Film aussieht?", fragte er.
„Besser", antwortete Tom. „Millionenfach besser."

8 The Millau Bridge

A. Text-based Tasks *page 56*

1
1. engineers architects
2. link Paris to the Mediterranean
3. it is one of the longest road bridges of its type and the single tallest road bridge in the world.
4. the surrounding landscape
5. to the environment

2
1. The traffic had to go down one side of the valley, cross the old bridge over the Tarn river, and then go up the other side of the valley.
2. There were terrible traffic jams particularly in the summer and this had a bad effect on the local villages and the environment.
3. It has shortened the journey by two hours.

3 *Possible questions:*
How long did it take you to plan and build the bridge?
When did the bridge open?
Who collaborated with you?
How high is the bridge?
How long is the bridge?
What are the important aspects of the design of the bridge?
How much impact did the construction have on the environment?

B. Use of Language *page 57*

1
1. A person who has a good reputation is respected.
2. To connect means to link or to bring two separate parts together.
3. An event which makes something happen.
4. Chaos is when there is complete disorder and confusion.

2
1. colourful
2. built
3. truth
4. failure
5. ruins
6. conquerors
7. demonstrations
8. was chosen
9. celebration
10. critical
11. combination
12. beautiful
13. questionnaire
14. were

C. Creative Writing *page 58*

1 1. You should make sure your front and back lights work. You should always wear a reflective band across your chest and back. It is even better to wear a reflective jacket. If you carry a backpack, choose one which has reflective bands on it. You should cycle near the side of the road so that cars can overtake you easily. *(60 words)*

3. The best thing to do is to look on the Internet for a list of canoeing clubs. Then choose a club in an area you like – maybe on the coast, or perhaps on a river - and phone them. Ask them if they do canoeing courses during the summer holidays and how much they cost. They will send you some forms to fill in. *(63 words)*

2 A The town where I live is quite small. It has an old part and a newer part. In the old part there are some buildings that are over four hundred years old. Most of them are made of red brick and wood. In one of them there is a museum where you can learn some very interesting things about the history of the town. In the other old buildings there are some nice little shops and an art gallery. This part of town is quite attractive for tourists.
I live in the newer part of town. The buildings there are more modern and practical. We have some large supermarkets, a cinema and a disco. I like my town because it offers something for everyone. *(124 words)*

B Yesterday morning my alarm didn't go off and I woke up late! I ran down the stairs, pulling on my clothes. I picked up my bag and raced to the bus stop. I was too late – the bus was disappearing down the road! So I started walking. Just then a car stopped and the driver asked me directions to Langley Sports Club. His face looked familiar. I explained how to get there and he handed me an envelope and said "Thanks very much. This is for you and a friend". Then he drove off. I opened the envelope. There were two tickets for Saturday's football match against Arsenal! What a stroke of luck that I got up late that day. *(120 words)*

D. Skills and Techniques *page 59–60*

1 1. Auf der Vorderseite der Euro-Noten findet sich die Darstellung eines Fensters oder eines Portals; auf der Rückseite sind Brücken abgebildet.
2. Im Februar 1996 fand ein Wettbewerb statt. 44 Entwürfe wurden eingereicht und im Dezember 1996 wählte eine 14-köpfige Jury den besten aus.
3. Robert Kalina war ein Künstler, der für die österreichische Nationalbank als Designer tätig war.
4. Die sieben Brücken stellen sieben Epoche der europäischen Geschichte dar – von der Römerzeit bis zur Gegenwart.
5. a) ein römischer Viadukt b) eine moderne Brücke
6. Die Fenster oder Portale symbolisieren die Kommunikation zwischen den europäischen Ländern.
7. Er wollte den Hinweis auf einzelne Mitgliedsländer vermeiden. Es ging darum, Brücken als völker- und länderverbindende Symbole abzubilden.

2 Der Architekt war Sir Normann Foster, der wahrscheinlich vor allem für seine Neugestaltung des Reichstags bekannt ist, und er wurde unterstützt von einem der ältesten und berühmtesten Bauunternehmen Frankreichs, das auch den Eiffelturm gebaut hat. Über 10 Jahre hat es gedauert, die Brücke zu planen und umzusetzen. Das Resultat, das im Dezember 2004 eröffnet wurde, ist eine der längsten Brücken dieser Art und die höchste Straßenbrücke weltweit.
Geplant war, Paris und das Mittelmeer durch eine Schnellstraße zu verbinden, aber der Fluss Tarn stellte ein ernsthaftes Problem dar.

Abschlussprüfung
Englisch

Realschule
Baden-Württemberg

Cornelsen

Abschlussprüfung Englisch
Realschule Baden-Württemberg

Erarbeitet von

Günter Hanisch
(Lerntipps und Beratung)
Dave Humphreys
(Texte: Sailing Teens, Earth Day, Surfing with Sharks, One Who Understands, Millau Bridge)
Rachel Thomas
(Übungen)

Beratung

Gabriele Künstler
Sibille Renz-Noll
Angelika Spitzmüller

Redaktion

Chris Caridia, Publishing Services, Berlin

Umschlaggestaltung

havemannundmosch, konzeption und gestaltung, Berlin

Layout und technische Umsetzung
Ingo Ostermaier

Bildquellen:

Alamy, Abingdon (GRFAT Eingangsseite Sydney Opera (M): Iconotec (RF); GRFAT 1 Nr. 4 WRITING unten re.: Brownstock Inc. (RF); GRFAT 2 Nr. 4 SPEAKING: Digital Vision (RF); **argus Fotoarchiv**, Hamburg (GRFAT 2 Nr. 2 MEDIATION bicyclists: Peter Frischmuth); **Corbis**, Düsseldorf (Titelbild bicyclist (M): Patrik Giardino); **Getty Images**, München (Titelbild highrise building (M): Bryan Mullennix; GRFAT 1 Nr. 2 LISTENING li.: National Geographic/Annie Griffiths Belt; GRFAT 2 Nr. 4 SPEAKING oben: Riser/Adrian Weinbrecht); **iStockphoto**, Calgary (GRFAT 1 Nr. 1 WORDS unten li.: Gene Chutka, unten re.: Jeffrey Smith; GRFAT 1 Nr. 3 Australia's most dangerous animals: susan flashman; GRFAT 1 Nr. 1 LISTENING oben: Carlos Santa Maria, omelette: Elnur Amikishiyev; GRFAT 1 Nr. 2 LISTENING re.: Chuck Babbitt; GRFAT 1 Nr. 3 LISTENING oben: Pali Rao, GRFAT 1 Nr. 4 WRITING screen (M): _zak, question mark (M): Zeffss1; GRFAT 2 Nr. 1 WORDS: Diane White Rosier; GRFAT 2 Nr. 4 SPEAKING: Chris Schmidt; GRFAT 2 Nr. 1 READING li.: Søren Sielemann, 2.v. li.: Rich Legg, Mitte Chris Schmidt, 2. v. re.: ronen, re.: Suzanne Tucker); **Picture Alliance**, Frankfurt/Main (GRFAT 2 Nr. 3 READING: empics); **Picture Desk**, London (GRFAT 2 Nr. 3 READING slumdog movie poster u. still: Film 4/Celador Films/Pathe International/The Kobal Collection); **Plainpicture**, Hamburg (GRFAT Eingangsseite jeans with map (M): Sina Preikschat); **Shutterstock**, New York (GRFAT 1 Nr. 1 WORDS oben: Rob Wilson; GRFAT 1 Nr. 1 LISTENING chicken salad: Robyn Mackenzie, pasta: Joe Gough, pork chop: Nayashkova Olga; GRFAT 2 Nr. 1 WORDS oben li.: Robert Ranson, oben re.: Rick Becker-Leckrone, unten li.: Amy Myers); **Theodora Children's Trust**, London (S. 18: www.theodora.org.uk); **vario images**, Bonn (GRFAT 2 Nr. 2 MEDIATION background bicycles: wave

Textquellen:

S. 12 *Global Pizza*. Reproduced by permission of Oxford University Press from New Headway Intermediate the new edition Students Book by John and Liz Soars © Oxford University Press 2003; S. 18 *The clown doctor*. Theodora Children's Trust, London, www.theodora.org.uk

www.cornelsen.de

1. Auflage, 2. Druck 2010

Druck: CS-Druck CornelsenStürtz, Berlin

ISBN 978-3-06-032296-1

Inhalt gedruckt auf säurefreiem Papier aus nachhaltiger Forstwirtschaft.

Inhalt

Liebe Schülerin, lieber Schüler,

Wie ihr wisst, steht am Ende der 10. Klasse eine schriftliche Prüfung im Fach Englisch.

Die Aufgaben in diesem Übungsheft richten sich nach der Form dieser Abschlussprüfung. Sie sollen dich – ebenso wie die folgenden Lerntipps – gezielt auf die Prüfung vorbereiten.

Die schriftliche Prüfung umfasst vier Aufgabenbereiche:

A. **Text-based Tasks** (Aufgaben zur Überprüfung des Textverständnisses)
B. **Use of Language** (Kontext bezogene Aufgaben zu Wortschatz und Grammatik)
C. **Creative Writing** (Verfassen eigener Textbeiträge)
D. **Skills and Techniques** (Anwendung erworbener Techniken und Fertigkeiten)

Die Arbeitszeit für die schriftliche Prüfung beträgt 120 Minuten. Du kannst 90 Punkte erreichen. Deine Rechtschreibleistung wird in den englischsprachigen Aufgabenteilen gewertet.

Der C-Teil (*Creative Writing*) ist besonders wichtig. Hier kannst du die meisten Punkte erreichen. Die Bewertung erfolgt nach inhaltlichen und sprachlichen Kriterien, die bei einer sehr guten Leistung so aussehen:

- *Inhalt entspricht den Anforderungen in besonderem Maße,*
- *erweiterter Wortschatz, idiomatische Ausdrucksweise,*
- *grammatikalisch korrekt und abwechslungsreich im Satzbau,*
- *sichere Rechtschreibung.*

Bitte unbedingt beachten: Bei inhaltlich oder situativ falscher Aussage gibt es für die gesamte Aufgabe 0 Punkte (selbst wenn sprachlich alles in Ordnung sein sollte!).

Beim zweiten Teil des *Creative Writing* gibt es zwei Möglichkeiten, auf die deutlich hingewiesen wird: *Choose task 2a)* ***or*** *2b). Do* ***not*** *work on both tasks.*

Wichtig ist, dass du die zur Verfügung stehende Arbeitszeit von 120 Minuten gut einteilst.

Du findest im Anhang dieser Lerntipps eine Liste von Arbeitsanweisungen, die häufig in Prüfungsaufgaben vorkommen. Bei der Lösung der Musteraufgaben dieses Heftes solltest du in der Liste nachschauen, wenn du eine Anweisung nicht verstehst oder wenn du ein wichtiges Wort vergessen hast.

Wenn du alle Musteraufgaben dieses Heftes bearbeitet hast, kannst du in Form der Selbsteinschätzung überprüfen, ob deine Fähigkeiten, Fertigkeiten und Kenntnisse wohl zu einer guten oder zufriedenstellenden Prüfungsleistung führen werden. (Siehe: *Teste dich selbst auf Seite 11.*)

Nun aber zu den einzelnen Aufgabenbereichen der Prüfung:

A. Text-based Tasks

Grundlage für verschiedene Arbeitsaufgaben ist der Basistext, den du stets auf der ersten Seite des Aufgabensatzes findest und der ungefähr 400 Wörter umfasst.

Beschäftige dich zunächst intensiv mit diesem Text. Gehe nicht zu schnell an die Arbeitsaufgaben auf den weiteren Seiten heran! Nicht nur im A-Teil, sondern auch in anderen Aufgabenteilen greift man nämlich immer wieder auf den Basistext zurück. Beispielsweise werden im B-Teil manchmal Aufgaben im Zusammenhang mit den im Basistext vorkommenden Wörtern gestellt. Außerdem wird in der Regel der Übersetzungstext des D-Teils dem Ausgangstext entnommen.

Lies also zunächst den Ausgangstext mindestens zweimal gut durch. Beim ersten Lesen wirst du herausfinden, wovon der Text handelt. Es ist ganz normal, wenn du nicht gleich alles verstehst. Beim zweiten oder dritten Lesen wirst du die Bedeutung vieler Wörter und Begriffe erschließen können, welche dir anfänglich unbekannt waren. Hilfreich ist es, wenn du dir überlegst, in welchem Zusammenhang die Wörter stehen, oder wenn du an die entsprechende Wortfamilie denkst. Häufig hilft die deutsche oder eine andere Sprache beim Verstehen des Begriffes.

Nach dem gründlichen Lesen und Erfassen des Textes kannst du an die Bearbeitung der Aufgaben gehen. Diese *text-based tasks* bestehen z. B. aus Fragen zum Ausgangstext. Die Antworten auf die Fragen können teilweise direkt dem Text entnommen werden. Die Reihenfolge der gestellten Fragen entspricht dabei der Reihenfolge der Textabschnitte. Bei den Antworten sind nur dann vollständige Sätze zu schreiben, wenn ausdrücklich darauf hingewiesen wird. (*Write in complete sentences.*)

Bei deinen Antworten auf die Fragen, die sich auf den Text beziehen, darfst du nicht zu viel dem Ausgangstext entnehmen. Du bekommst keinen Punkt, wenn du einen gesamten Textabschnitt abschreibst, nur weil du dort die richtige Antwort vermutest!

Manchmal beziehen sich nicht alle gestellten Fragen direkt auf den betreffenden Text. Dann wirst du darauf hingewiesen (*The answers needn't be in the text.*).

Gelegentlich sollst du angefangene Sätze mithilfe des Ausgangstextes vervollständigen: *Finish the sentences*. Oder du musst entscheiden, ob vorgegebene Aussagen, die sich auf den Text beziehen, richtig oder falsch sind: *Decide whether the following statements are right or wrong.*

Im A-Teil der schriftlichen Prüfung wird auch überprüft, ob du englische Fragen bilden kannst.

Häufig werden bei Aufgabenstellungen zur Fragebildung nur wenige Vorgaben gemacht, das heißt, dass du dir nicht nur überlegen musst, ***wie*** du den Partner fragen kannst, sondern auch, ***was*** du wissen möchtest:

> *You want to work as an au pair in Great Britain. Your pen friend from Manchester did so some time ago. Ask her or him about being an au pair. Use at least three different question forms.*

Beachte bitte den Hinweis im letzten Satz der obigen Arbeitsanweisung! Bildest du deine Fragen alle nach dem gleichen sprachlichen Muster, so verschenkst du Punkte.

Sobald du mit dem A-Teil fertig bist, solltest du alle Antworten durchlesen. Korrigiere die inhaltlichen und sprachlichen Fehler und achte besonders auf die Rechtschreibung. Bei falscher Schreibweise werden dir Punkte abgezogen! Wenn du dir nicht ganz sicher bist, ersetze das betreffende Wort durch ein anderes, das du besser kennst.

B. Use of Language

Im zweiten Teil der schriftlichen Prüfung werden Aufgaben zu Wortschatz und Grammatik gestellt (*Vocabulary – Grammar*).

Dabei handelt es sich um Einsetzübungen bei denen du die Wörter so in die Satzlücken einfügen musst, dass der Satz einen Sinn ergibt und alles sprachlich korrekt ist.

Bei den Aufgaben zur Überprüfung der Grammatik-Kenntnisse handelt es sich häufig um den richtigen Gebrauch der Zeitformen im Englischen (*use of tenses*). Die Schwierigkeit liegt u. a. in der unterschiedlichen Anwendung der einzelnen Zeitformen in den beiden Sprachen. Wo wir beispielsweise im Deutschen das Present Perfect verwenden (*Gestern bin ich daheim gewesen.*), steht im Englischen das *simple past* (*Yesterday I was at home.*).

Es lohnt sich, bei Aufgabenstellungen zum Gebrauch der Zeiten genau zu überlegen, in welchem zeitlichen Zusammenhang die entsprechende Aussage steht. Dazu empfiehlt sich die Suche nach typischen Signalwörtern, die meist einen eindeutigen Hinweis auf die richtige Zeitform geben. Im obigen Beispiel weist das Wort *yesterday* darauf hin, dass das *simple past* verwendet wird.

Wenn du in den folgenden Sätzen jeweils auf das Signalwort achtest, wirst du die Lösung leichter finden. (Allerdings wird das Signalwort in den Prüfungsaufgaben leider nicht unterstrichen sein – du wirst es selbst finden müssen!)

> *Please fill in the correct forms of the verbs given in brackets:*
> *My brother 1. … (go) to the same disco* ***every week***. ***Last week*** *he 2. … (meet) a girl called Vicky. He 3. … (not see) her at the disco* ***before***. ***On Monday*** *my brother 4. … (ask) Vicky to his 18th birthday party. It's next weekend. He 5. … (phone) her twice this week* ***so far***, *but she 6. … (not give) him an answer* ***yet***. ***Now*** *he 7. … (wait) for her to call.* ***If*** *she doesn't phone him soon, he 8. … (be) very sad.*

Im Prüfungstest sind die Aufgaben zu Wortschatz und Grammatik zu einer einzigen Übung zusammengefasst.
Dann ist es für das Textverständnis besonders wichtig, die Übung vor dem Ausfüllen der Lücken gut durchzulesen.

> *Read the text. Find suitable forms of the words and write them down.*
> *... Sometimes people ... (1. ask) me, "Why should I learn a foreign language? I'm not interested in ... (2. go) abroad anyway. I can't get the food I like, everything is ... (3. extreme) expensive, and people abroad usually ... (4. not/like) tourists anyway." – But even if you don't go abroad, languages are important. They've often been useful for me when I ... (5. must) talk to foreigners at work. And today, ... (6. watch) foreign TV programmes isn't ... (7. hard) with a satellite dish. Millions of people ... (8. do) it every year. Today videos and computer programmes help you to learn the pronunciation more ... (9. easy), which is important if you want to speak the language ... (10. proper).*

Bei anderen Aufgaben zum Wortschatz musst du häufig einen im Ausgangstext vorkommenden Begriff in einem Satz erklären. Beispiel: Du sollst in einem Text über den tropischen Regenwald den Begriff *forest* erklären. Das geht natürlich nur, wenn du weißt, dass *forest* im Deutschen „Wald" heißt.
Nun gibt es verschiedene Möglichkeiten, an die Aufgabe heranzugehen:

a) Du gibst eine Definition des Wortes *forest*: *A forest is a part of the landscape where you can find a lot of trees.*
b) Du versuchst, einen Satz zu bilden, aus dem klar ersichtlich wird, dass der Wald gemeint ist. (*The wood we need for making furniture is mainly cut in the forest.*)
c) Du erreichst die entsprechende Punktzahl auch, wenn du ein Wort mit gleicher oder ähnlicher Bedeutung (Synonym) als Erklärung heranziehen kannst (*Forest means woodland or woods.*).

Weitere Aufgaben geben Begriffe vor und du musst in einem angegebenen Textabschnitt ein Wort finden, das diesem in der Bedeutung am nächsten kommt (*Find words in the text that have more or less the same meaning.*) oder es wird das Gegenteil gesucht (*Find the opposites of the following words in the text.*).
Der umgekehrte Fall ist ebenso möglich, dass nämlich der Begriff aus dem Text genommen ist und du das entsprechende Wort aus deinem eigenen Wortschatz nennen musst. Achte dabei darauf, dass du im Text nochmals nachschaust, in welcher Bedeutung der Bergriff verwendet wurde. (*Find words or expressions that mean more or less the same. Find the opposites.*)

C. Creative Writing

Hier sollst du zeigen, wie gut du englische Texte schreiben kannst. Du sollst beispielsweise deine Meinung zu einem Thema schriftlich darlegen (*What's your opinion?*). Damit dir das gelingt, benötigst du einige wichtige Redewendungen:

Bei Zustimmung: *I agree (with the statement). – That's true. – That's right.*
Bei Ablehnung: *I can't agree (with ...). – That's not right. – I don't think you can say ... .*
Um die Meinung auszudrücken: *In my opinion ... . – I think ... .*
Für Begründungen: *First of all ..., second ..., and then/finally ... .*
Um die Meinung zusammenzufassen: *That's why ... . – To sum up, I would say ... .*

Denke daran, dass du deine Meinung begründen musst, wenn dies gefordert wird (*Give reasons.*).

Du möchtest das gleich einmal trainieren? Nun, dann schreibe z. B. deine Gedanken auf zu der Behauptung *Boxing is a bloodsport!* Entscheide dich zuerst, ob du diese Ansicht teilst oder ob du dem Boxsport gegenüber positiv eingestellt bist. Sammle dann Argumente für bzw. gegen das Boxen. Bringe diese Argumente in eine logische Reihenfolge und versuche Tatsachen und Beispiele zu finden, welche deine Meinung untermauern. Gehe erst danach an die schriftliche Ausarbeitung.

What would you do or say? ist eine weitere Aufgabenform, bei der du begründen sollst, wie du dich in einer bestimmten Situation verhalten würdest. Ein Beispiel aus dem Lehrbuch für Klasse 10:

You and a friend have planned an evening together. He/She tells you that he/she has invited someone else to join you – someone you don't like.

Du könntest diese Übung auch mit einem Partner durchführen und einen Dialog erarbeiten:
Die Arbeitsaufgabe: *Write a dialogue which solves the conflict.*

A: Excuse me, Sally. Have you got a minute?
B: Sure. What's up?
A: Well, I hate to say this, but ...

Im weiteren Verlauf des C-Teils musst du einen längeren Text verfassen. Oft lautet der entsprechende Hinweis: *Write about 120 words.* Dabei kann es sich um ganz verschiedene Textsorten handeln, z.B. um eine Geschichte, eine Nacherzählung, einen Bericht, einen Brief usw. So könnte ein Zeitungsbericht beginnen:

A woman's handbag was stolen yesterday in Church Street. The old lady had just left a shop when ...

Der Schluss des Zeitungsartikels lautet:
... The young man brought the handbag back to the old lady.

Deine Aufgabe ist es, den fehlenden Teil des Zeitungsartikels zu ergänzen.

Write a letter:

Diese Aufgabenstellung kommt in schriftlichen Prüfungen sehr häufig vor. Auch wenn du sie eventuell „abwählen“ kannst, solltest du wissen, wie ein formeller oder ein informeller Brief erstellt wird. Ein guter Weg, *formal letters* und *informal letters* voneinander abzugrenzen, wird in dieser Übung aufgezeigt:

There are two letters mixed up here. One is a formal letter to a computer firm. The other is an informal one to a friend. Underline the sentences that are from the formal letter. Then write the letter out.

Dear Sir or Madam,
Hi Amy!
Thanks for your e-mail. It really made me laugh!
I am writing about a computer that I bought from your company.
I'm sending you this note because my stupid computer isn't working.
I have had a lot of problems with it and when I phoned your hotline, I did not get any help.
I am very unhappy with this situation, and I think your company should help me more.
I phoned the hotline, but they were useless. A strange voice told me to press lots of buttons.
I've written a letter to the company. I hope they answer it.
I look forward to hearing from you.
I'll phone you at the weekend.
Lots of love,
Yours faithfully,
Mandy Hill
Mandy xxxx

Abschließend einige wichtige Hinweise zur Korrektur deiner selbst gestalteten Texte.

After you have written your text, take time to check it carefully. Go through the text several times; each time concentrate on something different, e.g.:

- *Check the* ***content****. Are all the ideas in it that you wanted? Does it make sense?*
- *Check the* ***grammar****. Pay special attention to tenses and word order.*
- *Check each* ***word****. Have you used the words correctly (e.g. the right prepositions with the verbs ...)? What about the spelling? (Here's a tip for checking the spelling: Read each word, one after the other, starting at the end of your text and going back to the beginning. Try it – it works!)*
- *Watch out for your* ***'favourite mistakes'****.*
- *If you can, put the text away some time and do something completely different. Then read your text again. You may see it differently – the way another reader would. And you may find mistakes you didn't see before.*
- *If necessary, rewrite your text. Practise correcting with every text you write.*

Häufige Fehler (*common mistakes*)

Nobody is perfect! Dennoch – es lohnt sich aufzupassen, vor allem im C-Teil der Prüfungsaufgaben. Dort kannst du zwar viele Punkte erreichen, wenn du über einen guten und abwechslungsreichen Wortschatz verfügst. Es dürfen allerdings nicht zu viele grammatische Fehler in den von dir verfassten Texten vorkommen.

In den folgenden 18 Sätzen ist jeweils ***einer*** der in Klassenarbeiten und bei Abschlussprüfungen häufig vorkommenden Fehler versteckt. Vermutlich wirst du viele Fehler entdecken, aber kannst du sie auch berichtigen? Versuche es!

1 *It gives a lot of interesting sights in London.*
2 *I've known my friend Tim since many years.*
3 *Betty is taller as Mandy, but Peggy is the tallest.*
4 *We mustn't hurry – there is enough time.*
5 *We go often to the zoo – it's not far from here.*
6 *The most kids wear jeans at our school.*
7 *She worked hardly – so she earned a lot of money.*
8 *Do you sometimes the washing-up at home?*
9 *My brother plays basketball very good.*
10 *Listen, your mobile phone rings; don't use it here.*
11 *These informations are interesting.*
12 *Her sister is nurse at the hospital over there.*
13 *Bob often play football on Saturday afternoon.*
14 *He was bitten from a dog, but he's feeling better now.*
15 *If you would play with your brother, he would be happy.*
16 *She enjoys to speak French.*
17 *We're here in town since last Friday.*
18 *People which drive too fast in a village are careless.*

Solltest du Probleme haben, die richtigen Lösungen zu finden, kannst du die Regeln in einem Grammatikbuch nachschlagen. Dort wird dir zum Beispiel erklärt, weshalb im Satz 10 die Verlaufsform stehen muss. Wenn du die Kompaktausgabe der *Cornelsen English Grammar* hast, kannst du im hinter der Lösung angegebenen Kapitel oder im Kapitel 20 (*common mistakes*) nachlesen. Auch im *Practice Book* zur *Cornelsen English Grammar* findest du in Kapitel 20 ähnliche Übungen. In beiden Ausgaben werden weitere häufige Fehler aufgezeigt, berichtigt und besprochen.

D. Skills and Techniques

Der D-Teil der Abschlussprüfung umfasst in der Regel eine Übersetzung sowie eine Übung zur Mediation. Unter Mediation versteht man die Übermittlung von Informationen. Es handelt sich dabei um die Übertragung vom Englischen ins Deutsche oder auch vom Deutschen ins Englische, wobei es um eine Übertragung geht, die eine sinngemäße Wiedergabe der Textinhalte oder einer Mitteilungsabsicht, aber keine wortgenaue Übersetzung verlangt.

Der Text, den du aus dem Englischen ins Deutsche zu übersetzen hast, wird in den meisten Fällen dem Ausgangstext auf Seite 1 der Abschlussprüfung entnommen. Dadurch ist er dir inhaltlich nicht mehr ganz fremd. In den vorhergehenden Teilen der schriftlichen Prüfung hast du dich bereits intensiv mit diesem Text als Ganzes befasst. Dennoch musst du beim Übersetzen einige wichtige Unterschiede im Gebrauch der beiden Sprachen beachten. Damit du das Übersetzen gleich ein bisschen üben kannst, werden die folgenden Hinweise teilweise auf Englisch gegeben:

- *word order:*
  They ***often get*** *into trouble. (Sie* ***geraten oft*** *in Schwierigkeiten.)*
- *different use of nouns, verbs, adjectives and adverbs:*
  He ***loves*** *taking photos. (Er macht* ***sehr gerne*** *Fotos.)*
- *prepositions:*
  Going ***to*** *museums can be fun. (Es kann Spaß machen,* ***in*** *Museen zu gehen.)*

– *different ways of saying things mean you can't translate word for word:*
  *They dress **the same way**. (Sie ziehen sich **gleich** an.)*
– *different use of tenses:*
  *We **didn't** understand. (Wir **haben nicht** verstanden.)*

Zu jedem der oben genannten Punkte eine kleine Übersetzungsübung:

1 Her brother came home **shortly before midnight yesterday**.
(*Beachte die unterschiedliche Satzstellung.*)

2 They **like** skiing. (*Ändere die Wortart bei like!*)

3 I watched the match **on** TV. (*Wähle eine andere Präposition.*)

4 It **took her** five minutes **to get there**. (*Übersetze nicht Wort für Wort.*)

5 **We'll** do that later. (*Verwende eine andere Zeitform.*)

Mediation

Hierbei wird von dir verlangt, dass du einen englischen Text (z.B. aus dem Internet) Informationen entnimmst und sie auf Deutsch weitergibst oder du musst zwischen einer deutsch- und englischsprachigen Person vermitteln.

Und nun: Viel Erfolg bei der schriftlichen Abschlussprüfung!

Anhang 1

Hier erhältst du eine Liste der Arbeitsanweisungen, die in Prüfungsaufgaben vorkommen. Wenn du eine Anweisung nicht verstehst oder ein Wort vergessen hast, kannst du hier nachschauen.

A-Teil:

Complete/Finish the sentences with information from the text.	Ergänze die Sätze mit Informationen aus dem Text.
Answer the questions.	Beantworte die Fragen.
The answers needn't be in the text.	Die Antworten müssen nicht im Text stehen.
You do not have to write complete sentences.	Du brauchst keine vollständigen Sätze zu schreiben.
Decide whether the following statements are right or wrong.	Entscheide, ob die folgenden Aussagen richtig oder falsch sind.
Give advice.	Gib Ratschläge.
Ask questions.	Bilde Fragen.

B-Teil:

Choose three of the following words and explain them in a complete sentence.	Wähle drei der folgenden Begriffe aus und erkläre in einem Satz, was diese bedeuten.
Name the things that are described here.	Benenne die hier beschriebenen Dinge.
Write complete sentences.	Schreibe vollständige Sätze.
Read the text and write down the suitable form of the words (given in brackets).	Lies den Text und schreibe die passende Form der (in Klammern angegebenen) Wörter.
Write down expressions from the text which mean more or less the same.	Schreibe Begriffe, die im Text vorkommen und die praktisch dieselbe Bedeutung haben.
Which expressions match the definitions below?	Welche Begriffe passen zu den unten stehenden Worterklärungen?
Find the opposites.	Finde die Gegensätze.

C-Teil:

Continue the dialogue.	Führe den Dialog weiter.
Give your opinion.	Lege deine Meinung dar.
What do you think of/about it?	Was denkst du darüber?
Write a possible ending to the story.	Schreibe ein mögliches Ende der Geschichte.
What do these signs here mean?	Was bedeuten diese Zeichen/Piktogramme?
What would you do or say?	Wie würdest du reagieren?
What would you suggest?	Was würdest du vorschlagen?
Make four suggestions.	Mache vier Vorschläge.
Write a a dialogue/a letter/a story.	Schreibe einen Brief/einen Dialog/eine Geschichte.
Explain yourself.	etwa: Erläutere, wie du reagieren würdest.
Give advice.	Gib Ratschläge.
Write sentences about your ideas.	Schreibe Sätze über deine Ideen/Vorstellungen.
Imagine ...	Stelle dir ... vor.

D-Teil:

Translate into German.	Übersetze ins Deutsche.
Pass on/Transfer the information.	Gib die Informationen weiter.
Mediation	Sprachmittlung

Teste dich selbst!

Bevor du an Aufgaben zur schriftlichen Abschlussprüfung herangehst, kannst du dich selbst prüfen, ob deine Fähigkeiten, Fertigkeiten und Kenntnisse zu einer guten Leistung führen. Kreuze hinter den folgenden Sätzen an, was bei dir immer, oft oder selten zutrifft.

Aufgabenteil A (Textverständnis): Ich kann ...	*immer*	*häufig*	*selten*
... schon beim flüchtigen Lesen des Textes herausfinden, worum es geht.	☐	☐	☐
... wichtige Informationen, die der Text bietet, schnell erkennen.	☐	☐	☐
... nach dem genaueren Lesen darlegen, was der Textautor sagen will.	☐	☐	☐
... entscheiden, ob bestimmte Aussagen im Text richtig oder falsch sind.	☐	☐	☐
... Fragen, die zum Ausgangstext gestellt werden, beantworten.	☐	☐	☐
... selbst Fragen bilden, die mit dem Inhalt des Textes zu tun haben.	☐	☐	☐

Aufgabenteil B (Wortschatz und Grammatik): Ich kann ...	*immer*	*oft*	*selten*
... Wörter finden, die gleiche oder ähnliche Bedeutung wie andere haben.	☐	☐	☐
... passende Wörter finden (z. B. das Hauptwort zu einem Zeitwort).	☐	☐	☐
... Wörter in einem Text ergänzen (z. B. Präpositionen wie *in*, *at*, *on*).	☐	☐	☐
... die Bedeutung von englischen Wörtern und Begriffen erklären.	☐	☐	☐
... erkennen, wann ein Adjektiv (*quick*) oder ein Adverb (*quickly*) steht.	☐	☐	☐
... Zeitformen richtig verwenden (steht *simple past* oder *present perfect*?)	☐	☐	☐

Aufgabenteil C (Erstellung von Texten): Ich kann ...	*immer*	*oft*	*selten*
... meine Meinung darlegen und sie begründen.	☐	☐	☐
... meine eigenen Gefühle und die meiner Mitmenschen beschreiben.	☐	☐	☐
... Vermutungen über einen Sachverhalt äußern.	☐	☐	☐
... Texte zusammenfassen, nacherzählen oder zu Ende schreiben.	☐	☐	☐
... Dialoge erfinden bzw. unvollständige Dialoge vervollständigen.	☐	☐	☐
... Briefe, Geschichten, Berichte, Zeitungsartikel u. Ä. schreiben.	☐	☐	☐

Aufgabenteil D (Arbeitstechniken und Fertigkeiten): Ich kann ...	*immer*	*oft*	*selten*
... in Alltagssituationen die Aufgaben des Sprachmittlers übernehmen.	☐	☐	☐
... die Rolle eines Interviewpartners übernehmen.	☐	☐	☐
... einem Text Informationen entnehmen und weitergeben.	☐	☐	☐
... einen deutschen Kommentar zu englischen Texten geben.	☐	☐	☐
... mit einem zweisprachigen Wörterbuch umgehen.	☐	☐	☐
... Texte aus dem Englischen ins Deutsche übersetzen.	☐	☐	☐

1 Global Pizza

So you thought the hamburger was the world's most popular fast food? After all, McDonald's Golden Arches span the globe. But no, there is another truly universal fast food, the ultimate fast food. It is easy to make, easy to serve, much more varied than the hamburger, can be eaten with the hands, and it is delivered to your front door or served in fancy[1] restaurants. It has been one of America's favourite foods for over 50 years. It is, of course, the pizza.

It is kind of silly to talk about the moment when pizza was 'invented'. It gradually evolved[2] over the years, but one thing is for certain – it has been around for a very long time. The idea of using pieces of flat, round bread as plates came from the Greeks. They called them 'plakuntos' and ate them with various simple toppings such as oil, onions, and herbs. The Romans enjoyed eating something similar and called it 'picea'. By about 1000 A.D. in the city of Naples, 'picea' had become 'pizza' and people were experimenting with more toppings: cheese, ham, anchovies, and finally the tomato, brought to Italy from Mexico and Peru in the sixteenth century. Naples became the pizza capital of the world. In 1889, King Umberto I and Queen Margherita heard about pizza and asked to try it. They invited pizza-maker Raffaele Esposito to make it for them. He decided to make the pizza like the Italian flag, so he used red tomatoes, white mozzarella cheese, and green basil leaves. The Queen loved it and the new pizza was named 'Pizza Margherita' in her honour.

Pizza migrated[3] to America with the Italians at the end of the nineteenth century. The first pizzeria in the United States was opened in 1905 at 53 ½ Spring Street, New York City, by Gennaro Lombardi. But the popularity of pizza really exploded when American soldiers returned from Italy after World War II and raved[4] about 'that great Italian dish'. Americans are now the greatest producers and consumers of pizza in the world. *(344 words)*

Pizza Trivia

- *Americans eat 350 slices of pizza per second.*
- *There are 61,269 pizzerias in the United States.*
- *Pizza is a $30 billion per year industry.*
- *October is national pizza month in the United States.*
- *The world's first pizzeria, the Antica Pizzeria Port'Alba, which opened in Naples in 1830, is still alive.*
- *Pizza Hut has over 12,000 restaurants and takeaway outlets[5] in over 90 countries.*
- *In America, pepperoni is the favourite topping.*
- *Anchovies is the least favourite.*
- *In Japan, eel[6] and squid[7] are favourites.*
- *In Russia, it is red herring, salmon and onions.*
- *In Brazil they like green peas on their pizza.*
- *In Australia the favourites are shrimp and pineapple.*
- *The French love bacon and crème fraîche on theirs.*
- *The English love tuna and sweetcorn.*

1 ***fancy*** *vornehm, schick*
2 ***to evolve*** *(sich) entwickeln*
3 ***to migrate*** *zuwandern, einwandern*
4 ***to rave*** *schwärmen*
5 ***takeaway outlet*** *Verkaufsstellen*
6 ***eel*** *Aal*
7 ***squid*** *Tintenfisch*

A Text-based Tasks 16 pts

1

Decide whether the following statements are right or wrong. 4 pts

	true	false
1. The pizza was invented when Italians emigrated to the USA.	☐	☒
2. The Americans have a pizza celebration every year.	☒	☐
3. The colours of the Italian flag were made after the famous red, white and green 'Pizza Margherita'.	☐	☒
4. More pizzas are eaten in the USA than anywhere else in the world.	☒	☐

2

Find the information in the text. Write complete sentences. 6 pts

1. Why is pizza even more popular than hamburgers? (three items)

It is more varied. easy to serve, easy to make, It is round

2. Who ate 'plakuntos' and 'picea'? (two items)

Romans and Greeks

3. Why was Naples famous 400 years ago? (one item)

The worlds first pizzaria opened in 1830 in Naples

3

Ask questions. 6 pts

*Your English friend has just come back from a holiday camp in the USA. Write **four** questions to ask him about the food and the meals there. Use at least **three** different question forms.*

1 What did you have ~~eat~~ in USA?

2 ~~How~~ was the pizza in USA good?

3 Which restaurant was you favourite?

4 What was better the pizza our the hamburgers?

B USE OF LANGUAGE 24 *pts*

1 *Vocabulary – Grammar*

Read the text. Find suitable forms of the words and write them down. 12 *pts*

Hi! My name is Dan. I'm eighteen and I'm a pizza (1.) deliver ________ boy. It is a great job but it is very (2.) ________. I deliver pizzas and then ride back to the pizza shop to collect more about ten times in one evening! I am used to all sorts of weather but I have to be (3.) angry ________ when it rains because the roads are (4.) slipy ________ and (5.) dangorous ________ Most customers are very (6.) ________ but some are (7.) friendly ________ because they take ages to find their purse. What I hate are dogs that bark at me (8.) ________ when I ring at the door. The part of the job I like (9.) ________ is (10.) ________ the names of all the roads. I (11.) ________ some very funny ones like Happy Street or Fish Bowl Lane up to now! When I finish work at about 11 pm, I (12.) ________ ! Guess what I have for dinner? Yes, a pizza!

1.	deliver	4.	slip	7.	annoy	10.	learn
2.	tired	5.	danger	8.	angry	11.	discover
3.	care	6.	friend	9.	good	12.	starve

2 *Write complete sentences to explain the meaning of* **three** *of the following words.* 9 *pts*

1. universal (line 2) universal calls all over the world.
2. toppings (line 12) Toppings are ingredients to fill for the pizza.
3. century (line 18) ________
4. capital (line 19) capital is a town, wher the president is

3 *Find the words in the text (see lines 6–13) that have more or less the same meaning.* 3 *pts*

1. step by step ________
2. different ________
3. nearly the same ________

C Creative Writing 27 pts

1 ***What would you do or say?*** *9 pts*
Choose **two** *of the situations and explain yourself. Write about 60 words altogether.*

1. On the bus you see a backpack on an empty seat.
2. A friend lends you a computer game. He wants it back and you can't find it.
3. You have been out with a friend and come home late. Your mother says you can't see any friends for the next two weeks.

2 *Choose task A* ***or*** *B. Write about 120 words altogether.* *18 pts*

A *Write a story on the topic of your choice using the following words. Find a suitable title.*

invented became famous the idea

B *Write an email.*

Your friend is interested in a restaurant that opened up a few weeks ago.
Give your impressions of the food, service, atmosphere, prices, etc.

D Skills and Techniques 23 pts

1 *Mediation* 11 *pts*

Im folgenden Text geht es um Gerichte, die in den USA sehr beliebt sind. Dein Freund, der kein Englisch spricht, hat zu diesem Thema die unten stehenden Fragen. Bitte beantworte sie auf Deutsch.

Ask for a hamburger, a sandwich, a hotdog, spaghetti and pizza almost anywhere in the world and you'll be understood! But strangely, this global food isn't modern at all – in fact, all these dishes have been around for a long time. Where did they originate? Well, it's pretty clear where the hamburger came from – Hamburg, in Germany, of course! When German immigrants from that city settled in New York in the early 1800's they introduced their speciality – cooked minced beef – to the Americans. To make it easier to eat, it was put in a 'bun' and today the hamburger has become the most popular fast food. Just like the hotdog – a long hot sausage in a bread roll – which originated in Frankfurt. In German it was called a 'dachshund' sausage, but once it was taken to the USA by German immigrants, Americans found it easier to call it simply a 'hot dog'! (Find out more on the website www.theholidayspot.com/hotdog).

The sandwich was invented by the Earl of Sandwich (Sandwich = a town in the south of England) in the eighteenth century because it was a quick and easy meal to eat while he was busy gambling!

Pizza and spaghetti were introduced to the world by the Italians who have been making these dishes for centuries. 'Pizza' means 'little pie' in Italian and spaghetti 'little cords'. Like the Germans, it was Italian immigrants in the USA who introduced their traditional dishes to the Americans. In fact, 'spaghetti' is just one of the hundreds of shapes of 'pasta' – an Italian word meaning a mixture of flour and water. Find out all about pasta shapes (macaroni, vermicelli, etc) and what their names mean on the website www.ilovepasta.org/shapes.

And for more information and history about all the dishes above, visit the website www.what'scookingamerica.net and click on 'History of Favourite Foods'.

Fragen

1. Aus welchen drei Ländern kamen die fünf in Zeile 1 erwähnten Gerichte ursprünglich? (2 Punkte)
2. Wie kamen Hamburger und Hot Dogs in die USA? (2 Punkte)
3. Warum werden Fleisch und Würstchen im Brötchen serviert? (2 Punkte)
4. Wo kommt der Name 'Sandwich' her? (2 Punkte)
5. Sind Pizza und Spaghetti moderne Gerichte? (1 Punkt)
6. Wie viele Pastaformen gibt es? (1 Punkt)
7. Woraus wird Pasta gemacht? (1 Punkt)

2 *Translate the following paragraph into German.* **12** *pts*

Pizza migrated to America with the Italians at the end of the nineteenth century. The first pizzeria in the United States was opened in 1905 at 53 ½ Spring Street, New York City, by Gennaro Lombardi. But the popularity of pizza really exploded when American soldiers returned from Italy after World War II and raved about 'that great Italian dish'. Americans are now the greatest producers and consumers of pizza in the world.

2 The Clown Doctor

All over the world, children in hospital are being treated with a new kind of medicine: laughter. Lucy is 23 and works for the Theodora Children's Trust. She is one of many clown doctors who bring a smile to the faces of sick children.

“I am a Theodora clown doctor. I call myself Dr. LooLoo. I spend two days a week in children's hospitals being extremely silly with my friend and colleague Dr. Chequers. We make funny faces, tell jokes, and do magic tricks. As I walk into the wards[1], I blow bubbles, shake hands with the kids, and make up nonsense songs for those children well enough to sing. We take special balloons to make 'balloon animals' and tell funny stories about them. We often meet kids who one week look really sick, then we go back the next week and they are racing about yelling: 'Hi there, Dr. LooLoo! Hi Dr. Chequers!'

I am naturally a very cheerful person. I have always been a clown. In fact, my father is a clown and I started working with him when I was eight years old. I knew it was just the job for me and I became a clown doctor because I think it is a great way to cheer up sick, frightened children in hospital. I wear a fancy coat, a yellow shirt, and tights with big stripes. Also, I have a red rubber nose and wear my hair in crazy plaits.

Being a clown in a hospital is very tiring both physically and emotionally. We have to learn not to show our feelings, otherwise we would be useless. Clown doctors are sensitive but this is not a side most people see. To the children we are happy all the time. I am still learning to allow myself to feel sad occasionally. There are special kids you get really close to. At the moment I am working with a very sick little girl from Bosnia who speaks no English, so our only common language is laughter. She has been in and out of hospital for operations so many times and she is always on my mind.

At lunchtime we eat in the hospital cafeteria and that is really useful because we meet the nurses and doctors. They tell us about particular kids who they think will benefit from[2] a clown doctor visit. If a child is frightened – perhaps they are being given an injection or some nasty medicine – we can distract them so the nurses can do their job.

At about six o'clock Dr. Chequers and I take off our make-up and change our clothes. We are totally exhausted. Sometimes I have a night out with friends. It helps me unwind[3]. When I finally fall into bed, I crash out[4]. At weekends we are often asked to participate in events to raise money for the Theodora Children's Trust. It is a charity so we are paid with the money people give. Being a clown doctor makes the worries of everyday life seem small. All in all, I feel privileged to do this job.” *(519 words)*

1 ***ward*** *Abteilung*
2 ***to benefit from*** *Nutzen ziehen aus, profitieren von*
3 ***to unwind*** *(sich) entspannen*
4 ***to crash out*** *hier: abschalten, sofort einschlafen*

A Text-based Tasks 16 pts

1 *Finish the sentences using information from the text.* 4 pts

1. Lucy has always wanted to be a clown ever since ...

2. Clown doctors can't show their real feelings because ...

3. Eating in the hospital cafeteria is useful because ...

4. When a child is frightened or worried, Lucy ...

2 *Answer the questions in complete sentences. The answers needn't be in the text.* 6 pts

1. What kind of person do you think Lucy is?

2. How do sick children feel when they watch a clown doctor?

3. What do the clown doctors often do at weekends?

3 ***Ask questions.*** 6 pts

You are interviewing Lucy, the clown doctor, about her work. Write ***four*** *questions to ask her. Use at least* ***three*** *different question forms.*

1

2

3

4

B Use of Language 22 pts

1 *Write complete sentences to explain the meaning of* ***three*** *of the following phrases.* 9 pts

1. make a funny face (line 15)

____

2. shake hands (line 17)

____

3. cheer up sick children (line 28)

____

4. get close to someone (lines 38–39)

____

2 ***Vocabulary – Grammar***
Read the text. Find the suitable forms of the words and write them down. 13 pts

A Passage to India

When I (1.) ____________ university last year, I couldn't decide what sort of job I wanted to do so I decided to go abroad for a year. One of my friends had just come back from India, where he (2.) ____________ in a village school just outside Delhi. I was (3.) ____________ by his (4.) ____________ of India. He told me about the children who lived in such (5.) ____________ but were so happy to go to school. His stories (6.) ____________ me so much that I was (7.) ____________ persuaded to go there myself. My friend (8.) ____________ to the school and told them I was the (9.) ____________ teacher and I sent them a letter with my photograph. I got a summer job and saved up enough money for the plane fare. I flew to India at the (10.) ____________ of September. As I stepped out of the plane at Delhi Airport into the dust and the (11.) ____________, I remember (12.) ____________ very excited. This was the start of an (13.) ____________ adventure.

1.	leave	5.	poor	8.	write	11.	hot
2.	teach	6.	interest	9.	replace	12.	feel
3.	fascinate	7.	easy	10.	begin	13.	excite
4.	describe						

C Creative Writing 27 pts

1 ***Describe a profession.*** *Write about 60 words altogether.* 9 *pts*

The Theodora Children's Trust asked you to look for a person who would join the hospital as a clown doctor. Write a job description to appear as an advertisement in the local newspaper. Don't copy from the text.

2 *Choose task A* ***or*** *B. Write about 120 words altogether.* 18 *pts*

A *Write a story.*

Imagine you were one of the children visited by Lucy. Write about what happened.

B *Write an article to promote*[1] *the Theodora Children's Trust.*

1 ***to promote*** *werben für*

D Skills and Techniques 25 pts

1 ***Mediation*** *13 pts*

You are in London with a friend who wants to find out about the Theodora Children's Trust. He is interviewing a spokesman who works for the Trust. Since your friend doesn't speak English very well, you will have to interpret his questions. Write down the questions in English and give the answers in German.

Your friend: Was genau macht der 'Theodora Children's Trust'?

You: ______________________________

Spokesman: It's an organisation that trains clown doctors and sends them to hospitals to cheer up sick children.

You: ______________________________

____

Your friend: Und wie lange gibt es ihn schon?

You: ______________________________

Spokesman: Over ten years. The very first clowns went to a big London children's hospital in 1994.

You: ______________________________

____

Your friend: Was lernen die Clown Doctors während ihrer Ausbildung?

You: ______________________________

Spokesman: They have medical training and learn how to deal with sick children. And artistic training teaches them all sorts of ways to entertain children.

You: ______________________________

____

____

Your friend: In wie vielen Krankenhäusern in Großbritannien kommen Clown Doctors zum Einsatz?

You: ______________________________

____

Spokesman: There are clown doctors in about ten major British hospitals at the moment.

You: ______________________________

____

2 *Translate the following paragraph into German.* 12 *pts*

Being a clown in a hospital is very tiring both physically and emotionally. We have to learn not to show our feelings, otherwise we'd be useless. Clown doctors are sensitive but this is not a side most people see. To the children we're happy all the time. I'm still learning to allow myself to feel sad occasionally. At the moment I'm working with a very sick little girl from Bosnia who speaks no English, so our only common language is laughter.

3 Surfing with Sharks

Great white sharks are famous for eating almost everything, and fishermen have found all sorts of things in their stomachs, from car tyres to cuckoo clocks. But experts say that great white and other large sharks are mostly fond of eating seals, sea lions and sea turtles. Many marine biologists think there may be an explanation why sharks attack surfers more often than they attack divers, swimmers or fishermen.

When surfers swim out to sea looking for a big wave, they move the surfboard over the water with their arms and legs. From below, where the sharks are, the surfers and their boards look similar to seals or sea turtles. Sharks don´t see very well, so they probably attack surfers by mistake. In fact, sharks almost never try to eat a surfer once they know that he or she is not their favourite food.

13-year-old Bethany Hamilton learnt a very hard lesson about sharks. Bethany, a champion surfer, was surfing with friends in Hawaii when, suddenly, a shark attacked. The 4.6-metre tiger shark took off her left arm and bit her shoulder and board. Fortunately, Bethany´s friends acted fast and saved her life. Now, after a series of operations, she has gone back to surfing, she has been on TV and in magazines, and some people in Hollywood are making a film about her story.

Bethany Hamilton was very lucky, and her future looks bright. But the future of sharks may not be so bright. Every year millions of sharks are killed because of cruel and irresponsible fishing practices. Of the 390 species of shark, eighteen species are considered seriously endangered, and this number is growing every year.

Surfing is becoming more and more popular all over the world: in the Canary Islands and California, in Australia and the Algarve, people are riding the waves. Experts say that surfers need to learn how to live with sharks, because we humans are really only visitors in the sharks' natural environment. The International Shark Attack File, an organisation that helps surfers and swimmers protect themselves from shark attacks, gives these tips:

! Never surf alone !
! Never surf at night or in dark waters !
! If you see a shark, stay calm and leave the area quickly and quietly !
! Always take a first aid kit with you when you go surfing !

If we learn to respect sharks, we will be able to surf safely. *(403 words)*

A TEXT-BASED TASKS 16 pts

1 *Decide if the following statements are right or wrong.* 4 pts

	true	false
1. Sharks often eat rubbish.	☐	☐
2. Sharks' eyesight is not good.	☐	☐
3. Fishing practices are responsible for killing millions of sharks.	☐	☐
4. The number of surfers has gone down over the last few years.	☐	☐

2 *Find the information from the text. Write complete sentences.* 6 pts

1. How many different types of shark exist?

____

2. Which organisation was set up to give surfers information about sharks?

____

3. What should you do if you are in the water and see a shark?

____

3 ***Ask questions.*** 6 pts

Bethany Hamilton is answering questions about her shark attack on an internet chat. Ask her ***four*** *questions about it. Use at least* ***three*** *different questions forms.*

1 ______________________________

2 ______________________________

3 ______________________________

4 ______________________________

B Use of Language 21 pts

1 Vocabulary – Grammar

Read the text. Find siutable forms of the words and write then down. 12 pts

Panbanisha looks like an ordinary chimpanzee but, in fact, she is a chimp with a (1.) ________________!

She is unique because (2.) ________________ have trained her to speak English! She doesn't actually speak – she types words onto the computer and the computer voice (3.) ________________ speaks them. Her computer has a (4.) ________________ designed keyboard and each key is (5.) ________________ with a symbol which represents words such as 'apple', 'hot', 'tired'. Panbanisha has learnt 5,000 English words so when she is (6.) ________________ hungry she can say to her (7.) ________________ 'Please get me a sandwich', and if she's (8.) ________________, she says, 'Bed, please'. At first her trainers were (9.) ________________ that she would confuse words and would be not be able to say anything. But she has an excellent memory and can express (10.) ________________ very well. One hot day last summer, for example, after Panbanisha (11.) ________________ the coins she had been given as a reward for learning new words, she said in sign language, 'I'm (12.) ________________! Please buy me a pool. The money is in my purse.'

1.	different	4.	special	7.	keep	10.	oneself
2.	science	5.	mark	8.	sleep	11.	save
3.	automatic	6.	feel	9.	worry	12.	boil

2

Write complete sentences to explain the meaning of ***three*** *of the following phrases.* 6 pts

1. fond of (line 5) ________________
2. marine biologist (line 6) ________________
3. fishing practices (line 37–38) ________________
4. a first aid kit (line 54) ________________

3

Find the words in the text which mean the ***opposite*** *of the words below.* 3 pts

1. above (lines 10–17) ________________
2. easy (lines 18–27) ________________
3. getting smaller (lines 34–44) ________________

C Creative Writing *27 pts*

1 ***What would you do or say?*** *9 pts*

Choose **two** *of the following situations and explain yourself. Write about 60 words altogether.*

a) You're standing on the beach and you see someone in difficulty in the sea.

b) You spent all evening learning a page of your geography book for a test next day. In the morning you realize you have been studying the wrong page.

c) You've forgotten your key and nobody's at home.

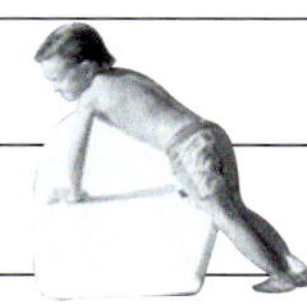

2 *Choose task A* ***or*** *B. Write about 120 words altogether.* *18 pts*

A *Write a diary entry.*

You went for a holiday at the sea. One day you tried to learn windsurfing. It was difficult! Write in your diary about that particular day.

B *Write a story.*

Write a story using the following words:

wallet | address | reward

Start like this: I was walking to my friend's house the other day when I saw …
and finish up like this: Ten pounds! More than a month's pocket money!

D Skills and Techniques 26 pts

1 *Mediation* 14 pts

Deine Freundin / dein Freund interessiert sich für den Surfsport. Sie / er versteht den Text nicht so gut und bittet dich daher, die unten stehenden Fragen zu den Informationen aus dem Internet auf Deutsch zu beantworten.

Today surfing is an international sport and there are major surfing events all over the world in countries which have ocean coastlines and high waves – e.g. South Africa, Australia, California, Indonesia, the French Atlantic Coast and many other places. But how did surfing start? Many people believe it started in Hawaii – a tiny island chain in the Pacific Ocean. Centuries ago, 'riding the waves' was the traditional pastime of the local fishermen who sat or stood on boats shaped like long wooden boards. Great importance and power were given to skilful wave riders and only the élite were allowed to surf along the best shores. When Captain Cook discovered Hawaii in 1778, he recorded seeing the native Hawaiians surf-riding and was impressed by their skill. In 1959 the island officially became the last state of the United States of America and the American way of life has now taken over. However, some Hawaiian traditions still remain. One of them, of course, is surfing and Hawaii is considered to be the best place in the world to 'catch a wave'. And when the surfing's finished for the day, surfers can indulge in another Hawaiian tradition, the Luau; a celebration of feasting and dancing with traditional food like roasted pig and sweet potatoes, and the traditional drink called 'Mai Tai'. Every guest is given a garland of flowers or shells and the women and girls dance in the traditional way.

Fragen

1. Was braucht ein Land, um gute Surf-Bedingungen zu bieten? (2 Punkte)
2. Welche Länder bieten solche Bedingungen? (4 Länder) (2 Punkte)
3. Wo liegt Hawaii? (1 Punkt)
4. Wie hat das Surfen vermutlich angefangen? (2 Punkte)
5. Durften damals alle überall mitsurfen? (1 Punkt)
6. Was ist 1778 geschehen? (1 Punkt)
7. Was hat Captain Cook auf Hawaii beobachtet? (1 Punkt)
8. Was ist 1959 geschehen? (1 Punkt)
9. Wie hat sich Hawaii nach 1959 geändert? (1 Punkt)
10. Was bekommen die Gäste beim ‚Luau'? (2 Punkte)

2 *Translate the following paragraph into German.* **12** *pts*

When surfers swim out to sea looking for a big wave, they move the surfboard over the water with their arms and legs. From below, where the sharks are, the surfers and their boards look similar to seals or sea turtles. Sharks don't see very well, so they probably attack surfers by mistake. In fact, sharks almost never try to eat a surfer once they know that he or she is not their favourite food.

4 EARTH DAY

Imagine a day when millions of people from about 200 countries around the world come together to celebrate and protest with a single purpose in mind. This is just what happens on April 22nd. The day is Earth Day, and the purpose that the people have in mind is to work for a healthier and safer world for everyone. It is the biggest celebration of its kind in human history.

Earth Day marks the anniversary of the birth of the modern environmental movement. In 1962 Gaylord Nelson, a US Senator, looked at the world around him and saw lakes and rivers polluted by rubbish and chemicals, forests that were slowly being destroyed every day, and towns and cities full of smog and car exhaust. Senator Nelson felt that the government was not doing nearly enough to protect the environment. So he spent the next eight years travelling round the USA and talking to all sorts of people about pollution and other dangers that were harming the planet.

Finally, on April 22nd, 1970, Senator Nelson and a group of university students organized the first Earth Day. The event was much more successful than the organizers had ever expected: over 20 million people – young and old, rich and poor, city people and country people – took part.

Today Earth Day is celebrated all over the world, and some countries even celebrate Earth Week, the week before April 22nd, and Earth Month throughout the whole month of April. Over 5,000 different environmental organizations are connected by the Internet, and they help people in their communities to plan demonstrations, campaigns, talks and other activities. But the idea is the same as it was in 1970: millions of people from all over the planet, rich and poor, old and young, want to build a healthier and safer world.

The problems that Gaylord Nelson saw everywhere in the 1960s still exist, and now we know about things like global warming and acid rain that most people could not even imagine 40 years ago. We need Earth Day today more than ever. So what can we do? Many young people participate in Earth Day through their schools. They organize clean-up campaigns or pick up rubbish in their communities. Others write letters to their local council asking for more environmental protection laws. Still others organize marches to promote recycling and other energy-saving activities. But perhaps the best way to celebrate Earth Day is to follow the organizers' advice: "Do something nice for the Earth, have fun, meet new people, and make a difference." *(427 words)*

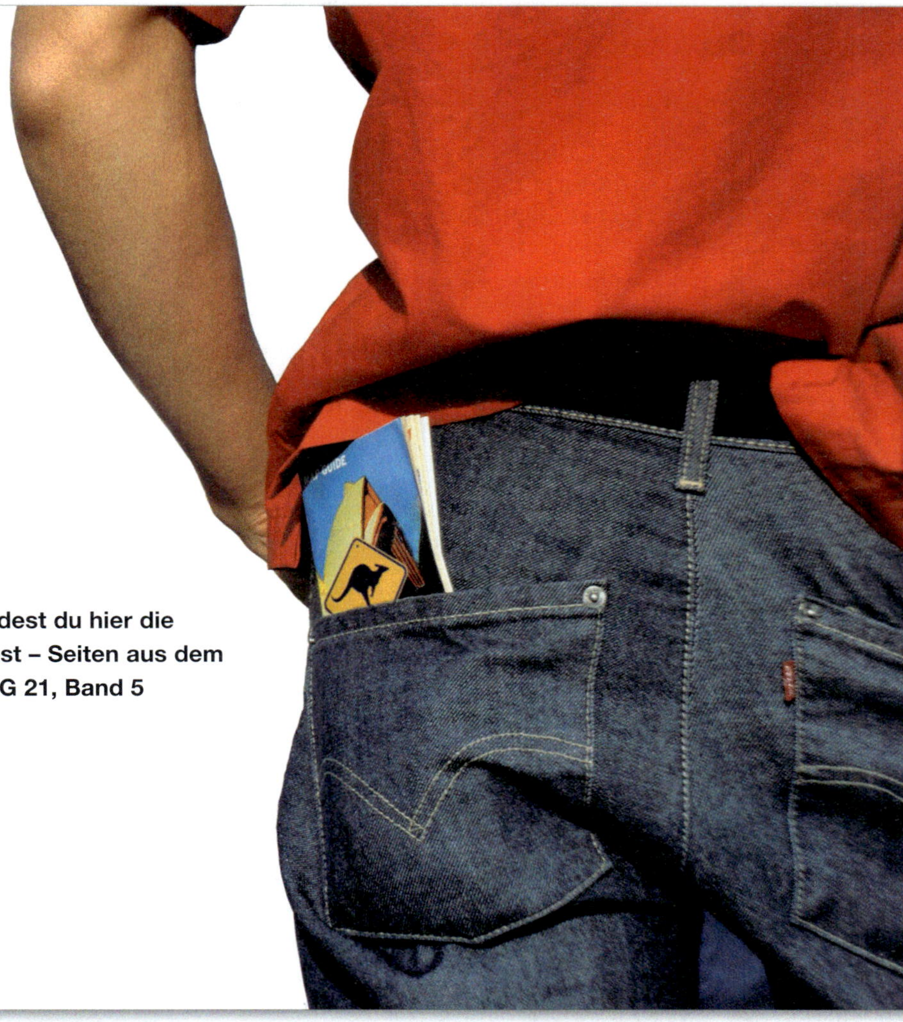

Zur Wiederholung findest du hier die Getting ready for a test – Seiten aus dem Schülerbuch English G 21, Band 5

1 WORDS Travelling

Fill in the right words to complete the sentences.

You're flying to Australia for a wonderful holiday. At the airport, you first (1) *check in*. Then you go to the (2) ... For your flight it's gate D21.

Now you're on the plane. The flight to Australia is very long and on the way you need to eat and drink. The flight attendant offers you a drink and a hot (3) ... There are lots of nice things on the menu today.

breakfast • (to) change planes • (to) check in • city centre • departure gate • key card • (to) land • meal • single ticket • suitcases • taxi • ticket machines

After you (4) ... at Singapore Airport, you finally (5) ... in Sydney. Of course, you hope that your (6) ... arrive too! If not, you'll have to go to the lost luggage office.

So how do you travel from the airport into the (7) ...? Well, the quickest and easiest way is to take a (8) ..., but it's also the most expensive one: it costs about 50 Australian dollars. So you decide to take a train instead. The (9) ... are easy to use and a (10) ... to the city is only 15 Australian dollars.

Now – tired but happy – you're at your hotel. The receptionist gives you the (11) ... to your room and tells you about the hotel – for example, the times when you can have (12) ... in the mornings.

2 Judy's job (Simple present and present progressive)

a) *Judy is the flight attendant who you can see in the photo above. Finish these sentences about her job. Use the **simple present** or the **present progressive**.*

1 Judy's job is exciting. She often ... (travel) to different countries.
2 Right now, she ... (fly) to Australia.
3 A typical day for Judy starts early. She usually ... (get up) at 5 o'clock. Then she ... (have) her breakfast and ... (drive) to the airport.
4 It is 10 o'clock now and Judy ... (work). She ... (bring) coffee and tea to the passengers on her plane.
5 Now it is 10 o'clock the next morning. Judy ... (just/arrive) at her hotel.
6 Judy always ... (stay) at a hotel when she is in another country. She ... (sleep) at the hotel – then the next day she ... (fly) home again.

b) *Write sentences about things that you often do and some things that you're doing right now.*
I often surf the internet. Right now, I'm chatting with my friends.

3 Australia's most dangerous animals (Simple past and past progressive)

Read the text about Australia's most dangerous animals on the right, then complete the two stories below. Use the simple past or past progressive of the verbs in brackets.

AUSTRALIA is home to some of the world's most dangerous animals. There are snakes, spiders and sometimes sharks. The most dangerous of all, however, are crocodiles. Two or three people die every year in crocodile attacks.

There's a crocodile in our tent!

In January 2005, two young Australians went camping near the Pentecost River in the north of Australia. At about 2 o'clock in the morning, they (1) *were sleeping* (sleep) when suddenly a crocodile (2) ... (come) into their tent. They (3) ... (run) to their car and (4) ... (climb) onto it. The next morning at 11 o'clock, they (5) ... (still/sit) on their car when some hunters (6) ... (arrive) and (7) ... (save) their lives.

Smile please!

In 2008, a tourist in Queensland was stupid – but lucky. He (8) ... (sit) in a boat on a river when a crocodile (9) ... (swim) towards the boat. The man's friend (10) ... (stand) on land. 'Put your hand in the water and play with the crocodile!' he (11) ... (shout). 'I'm going to take a photo.' Seconds later, the crocodile (12) ... (try) to bite the man's hand. 'It was a scary moment!', he (13) ... (say) afterwards.

4 WORDS It was scary! (Words that describe experiences)

a) *Look at the box with adjectives. Find five pairs of adjectives that mean (almost) the same: good – ...*

b) *Find at least eight pairs of adjectives that mean opposite things: amazing – bad; awesome – ...*

c) *Write six sentences using adjectives from the box:*

1) Yesterday I played table tennis against my younger brother and lost 11–2. It was depressing!
2) ...

amazing • awesome • awful • bad • boring • cool • crazy • dangerous • depressing • different • difficult • easy • excellent • exciting • fantastic • fine • funny • good • great • horrible • interesting • laughable • mad • nice • OK • sad • scary • silly • strange • surprising • terrible • unbelievable

5 WRITING One day last year ...

a) *Below is a very short story! Can you make it more interesting? Write the story again.*

Jake was riding his bike in the mountains. He fell off and broke his leg. He called for help with his mobile phone. Some people saved him. He went to hospital. He met Anne, a doctor. They fell in love. They got married.

When?	one day last year, last September, first, then, next, after that, finally, ...
Who?	the man/woman/people who ...
How?	quickly, slowly, suddenly, ... (really) amazing/awful; (feel) happy/sad, ...
Linking words	because, but, so (that), although, when, while, ...

b) *Compare your story with a partner's.*

1 LISTENING Travelling to Australia

oder Web-Code: EG21-B5-028

You are flying to Australia with your family.
- *Look at the questions below. You have 30 seconds.*
- *Listen to five announcements or short conversations that you hear on your journey. Note down the right answer –* A, B *or* C.
- *You will hear all the recordings* ***once***.

1 At Heathrow Airport in London you hear this announcement: 'Flight Q201 to Sydney is now boarding at ...'

A GATE 7 B GATE 17 C GATE 70

2 On the plane from London to Sydney, the flight attendant is offering you ...

A an omelette or pasta.

B chicken with a salad or pork chops.

C chicken with a salad or pasta.

3 At Sydney Airport one of your suitcases is missing! The lost luggage office is ...

A just over there. B on the first floor. C next to the passport office.

4 A taxi from the airport into the city costs ...

A AU$ 50 B AU$ 52.50 C AU$ 55.20

5 Now you are at your hotel. Tomorrow breakfast is from ...

A 06:00–10:00 B 06:30–9:30 C 07:00–10:30

2 LISTENING Shark attack!

oder Web-Code: EG21-B5-029

You are going to hear a radio news programme about how Jon Kerry, a young Australian, was attacked by a great white shark.

– *Look at the questions below for 30 seconds.*
– *Now listen and do the tasks. You will hear the news programme* ***twice****.*

a) *Which is right? Write down* A, B, C *or* D.

1 Jon was attacked near a beach in …
A Queensland.
B South Australia.
C New South Wales.
D Western Australia.

2 When he was attacked, Jon was …
A surfing.
B swimming.
C sunbathing.
D windsurfing.

3 The shark bit into Jon's …
A arm.
B foot.
C shoulder.
D leg.

4 It held him for around …
A 3.5 seconds.
B 5 seconds.
C 40 seconds.
D 5 minutes.

5 After the attack …
A a boat saved Jon in the water.
B the shark pulled Jon to the beach.
C Jon swam back to the beach.
D a big wave carried Jon to the beach.

6 Jon thought this was the … part.
A most exciting
B easiest
C scariest
D most painful

b) *Finish the sentences.*

1 Jon's friends probably saved his life when they … a rope[1] round his … and stopped the bleeding.
2 Jon is lucky. He will always have a big scar[2] but he …
3 Experts say that sharks don't normally …
4 The experts also say that more people die in road accidents in Australia … than from shark attacks …
5 You should always swim … so your friends can help you. And never swim … or … because that's when sharks usually feed.

[1] rope [rəʊp] *Seil* [2] scar [skɑː] *Narbe*

3 LISTENING Young Australians and the internet

oder Web-Code: EG21-B5-030

Young Australians are among the world's biggest users of the internet. Six Australian students are discussing what they do online.
- *Look very carefully at the statements below for 30 seconds.*
- *Now listen and do the task.*
- *You will hear the recordings only **once**.*

Right or wrong? True or false? Note down 'T' or 'F'.

1. Student 1 thinks that she spends too much time online.
2. Student 2 never does just one thing at a time when he uses a computer.
3. Student 3 thinks her parents don't care about what she does online.
4. Student 4 thinks that young people know how to be safe online.
5. Student 5 tells a story about something that happened to him.
6. Student 6 thinks the internet is good for teenagers.

4 WRITING An online magazine for young Europeans

You often read an online magazine for young Europeans. This week, the magazine wants readers' ideas about the internet and it has a story competition.
Write about one of the two topics below. Write a text of about 150 words.

Topic 1: The internet and me
When and where do you usually use the internet? What do you do online? What things do you do most often online? Can the internet be bad for you?

Topic 2: A scary moment!
Finish this story in your own words.

It was a Saturday afternoon in September. I was bored, so I decided to go for a bike ride. After about an hour, I was on a small road in the country ...

How am I doing?

Check your answers to tasks 1–3 in the Answer key.

About the test

This test gave you the chance to try some of the kinds of tasks that you will have to do in your exam (*Abschlussprüfung*). If you found some tasks difficult, don't worry. You've got lots of time to practise. Remember: 'Practice makes perfect!'

Listening

The first three tasks in the test were listening tasks. The following questions will help you to think about how you did. Read the questions and tick the boxes that are right for you.

1 **How hard or easy was each task?**

	easy	OK	quite hard	very hard
Task 1	❑	❑	❑	❑
Task 2	❑	❑	❑	❑
Task 3	❑	❑	❑	❑

2 **What was difficult in the tasks?**

People spoke quickly. ❑
I found the accents difficult. ❑
There was a lot of information.
I couldn't find the exact answers. ❑
I didn't have time to write the answers to the questions. ❑
There were words and phrases that I just couldn't understand. ❑

3 **How did you do the tasks?**

I read the questions carefully first so I knew exactly what I had to listen for. ❑
I looked quickly at the questions first but only read them carefully while I was listening. ❑
I wrote as many answers as I could the first time I heard the text and checked them (or filled in gaps) the second time. ❑
There were lots of things I couldn't understand and I panicked. ❑

Writing

The fourth task in your test was a writing task. Work with a partner. Exchange the texts you've written and read your partner's text. Copy and fill in the assessment sheet[1] below. Remember: the idea is to help your partner with your feedback!

Assessment sheet				
Name of partner ...	☺	😐	☹	Comments
Did your partner ...				
1 ... write an interesting text / story?				
2 ... make grammar mistakes (with a tense, a plural form, etc.)?				
3 ... use interesting vocabulary or just easy words and phrases?				
4 ... write longer sentences with linking words or just short sentences?				
5 ... write a text that is clear and easy to understand?				

[1] assessment sheet *Beurteilungsbogen*

1 WORDS Free-time activities

What do you do in your free time? Are you sporty? Is running your hobby? Or do you like reading a good book?

a) *Work with a partner. How many free-time activities can you add to the list below?*

horse riding • drawing and painting • listening to music • playing a musical instrument • watching TV or DVDs • playing basketball • playing football • cycling • using a computer • reading books or magazines • relaxing • meeting friends • ...

b) *Look at your list and put the activities into groups.*

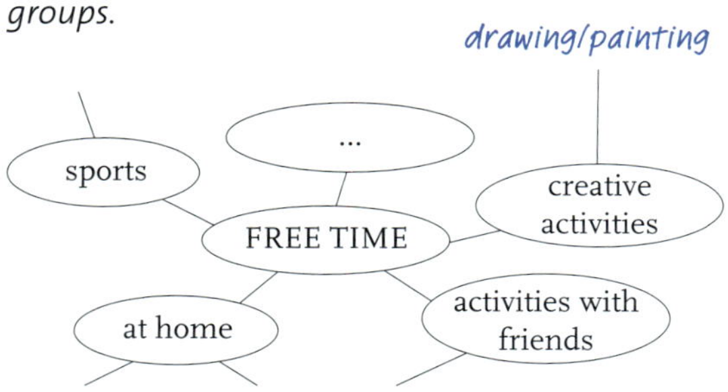

c) *Talk about all your free-time activities. Tell each other why you like/don't like doing them.*

A: I often go horse riding. I love horses and I think it's great to be with them every day.

B: Well, maybe, but it sounds like a lot of work. But I enjoy listening to music ...

2 WORDS Talking about films

You see this film review on a movie website. Find the missing words and phrases to complete the text.

(to) act • actor • drama • famous • main character • star • (to) take part in • talent • (to) tell the story • true events

Take the Lead * * * * *

'Ballroom dancing meets New York's gangs'
The (1) *drama* *Take the Lead* (2) ... of Pierre Dulaine, a ballroom dance teacher, who goes to work in one of New York's most difficult inner city schools full of problem kids. *Take the Lead* is actually based on (3) ..., and Pierre Dulaine is, in fact, a real person. He still works with American teenagers around the USA and has become quite (4) ... since the film came out.

The (5) ... of the film is the Spanish American (6) ... Antonio Banderas. He plays the (7) ... Pierre Dulaine. When Dulaine first arrives in the school, the kids all think he is crazy. They are into hip hop, not classical dance. However, after Dulaine shows them a tango with another professional dancer, the kids start to get interested. The film ends when they all (8) ... a national ballroom competition.

The kids are all 'normal' American teenagers and had never (9) ... before. But they are all natural acting (10) ... and some of them are amazing hip hop dancers.

In 2006, *Take the Lead* won an award for 'Best Teen Movie.'

3 I'd love to be a movie star (Conditional sentences type 2)

Finish these sentences about being a famous movie star. All the sentences are conditional sentences type 2.

1. If a famous director *chose* (choose) me for one of his films, I*'d / would be* (be) famous too.
2. I ... (go) to Hollywood if I ... (become) a famous actor.
3. I ... (not live) here if I ... (be) rich.
4. If I ... (act) in a movie, all my friends ... (come) to see me.
5. If I ... (have) lots of money, I ... (buy) a yacht.
6. If I ... (play) a part in a movie, I ... (meet) famous actors every day on the film set.
7. But the problem is, if I ... (be) a movie star, I ... (not see) my family very often.
8. Perhaps I ... (not be) so happy if I ... (be) a film star!

4 SPEAKING Having a conversation

Talk to your partner for about two minutes about something that interests you – films, magazines, music, what you did last weekend, the town where you live, ... The phrases below will help you.

starting a conversation	Hello. / Hi. / My name's ... / What's your name? / ...
likes and dislikes	I like / don't like ... / What about you? / And you? / ...
showing interest	Really? / Oh, that's interesting! / Sounds great! / Wow! / ...
agreeing and disagreeing	Yes, me too. / That's right! / Oh, I don't. / Sorry, I don't agree. / ...
asking questions	So when did you ...? / Why ...? / How long ...? / Where ...? / Sorry, can you say that again please? / ...
ending the conversation	See you soon. / Bye!

5 WORDS Jim and Kate (Words that describe feelings)

a) *Complete these sentences with words or phrases from the box on the right.*

angry • be afraid • be mad about sb./sth. • bored • confused • cool • different • excited • great • happy • independent • jealous • lonely • (to) look forward to sth. • nervous • proud • relaxed • responsible (for) • sad • safe • scared • shy • silly • strange • surprised • terrible • tired

1. Jim and Kate have been together for a month now and they ... still ... each other.
2. Kate was ... when Jim asked her if she'd like to date him. She thought he liked Laura.
3. Jim is usually very ..., so he wasn't even nervous on their first date.
4. But when Kate left his MP3 player on the bus last week, he was very ... with her.
5. Sometimes Kate is ... when Jim tries to be funny – his jokes are very strange!
6. At first she didn't want to meet Jim's parents as she always feels a bit ... with new people.
7. When Kate met her old boyfriend Pete at a party, Jim was a bit ... at first – until he saw that she wasn't interested in Pete any more.
8. They're ... the summer holidays this year: they're going to Canada for three weeks!

b) *Write six sentences like these with words you haven't used in a).*

1 READING Choosing a book

These American high school students are in their English literature class. They have to choose a book to read. To help them, their English teacher has written short summaries of some books.

Look at the profiles of the five students and the seven book summaries below. Choose the best book for each student.

Answer: Student A – Book ...

Student A : Conrad

Conrad doesn't really enjoy reading short stories or novels, but he reads magazines. He loves sport and is also interested in music and skateboarding.

Student B : Brittany

Brittany has her own blog where she writes her thoughts. She is fascinated by young people, their loves and fears, their relationships, and their problems.

Student C : Jeanette

Jeanette loves reading stories. For her, a 'good book' is one where the characters have lots of real life adventures. She doesn't like fantasy or horror stories.

Student D : John Paul

John Paul is interested in football but the thing he likes best is computer games. He particularly loves fantasy games where 'anything is possible'.

Student E : Ricky

Ricky's family came to the U.S. from Puerto Rico. Now, as a teenager, he is interested in politics and wants to help people from ethnic minorities.

BOOK SUMMARIES

Fiction

1 **Dark Universe** Three teenage friends fall through a 'time hole' and find themselves in a parallel world where amazing and fantastic things happen. Can they survive – and will they ever return to their old lives?

2 **Something** Something is 'out there'. Waiting. Watching. Looking for you! VERY scary!

3 **Lola and the Detective Agency** When Lola and her friends discover a crime, nobody believes them. They have to set up their own detective agency to catch the criminals. Lots of action right up to the last page!

Non-fiction

4 **Voices from the fields** Fascinating interviews with migrant workers from Mexico who talk about their lives in the fields of California where they pick fruit.

5 **Strategies for teens** Being a teenager is not always easy but this book is full of great advice about families, boy/girlfriends and many other aspects of teen life.

6 **The Journey West** The book uses diaries, letters and old photos to tell the fascinating story of the long journeys to the West in America's history.

7 **Babe** Babe Ruth was probably the greatest baseball player who has ever lived. This biography tells the true story of his life. Wonderful descriptions of exciting games!

2 MEDIATION A note to your friend

Your American friend is staying with you in Germany at the moment. Your friend would like to know about some interesting things to do.

Read the brochure below and write a short note in English to your friend. Give the main points about the tour. Use the example on the right to help you.

Hi!
Hope you slept well. You wanted to know about some interesting things to do while I'm at school. I found out about some guided cycle tours that sound great. Here are the main points:
–
–

Erleben Sie die Stadt per Rad

Fahrrad-Stadtrundfahrten

Fahrrad-Rundfahrten durch die Stadt – für Gruppen von 10–15 Personen – begleitet von erfahrenen Stadtführern.

Sehen Sie unsere Stadt und ihre Attraktionen vom Fahrrad aus. Wir machen Halt an interessanten Punkten. Dort werden Sie Informationen über die Geschichte der Stadt und touristische Highlights erhalten.

Dauer
Unsere abwechslungsreiche Tour führt durchs Stadtzentrum und verschiedene Stadtteile und dauert ca. 120 Minuten, in denen wir etwa 12 km zurücklegen.

Abfahrt
März – September
täglich 10:00 und 14:00 Uhr.

Treffpunkt ist vor dem Informationszentrum neben der Liebfrauenkirche im Stadtzentrum (bei schlechtem Wetter im Informationszentrum).

Preise
€ 29,– pro Person inkl. Fahrradmiete
(Bei angemeldeten Gruppen mit mehr als 25 Teilnehmern € 22,50 pro Person.)

3 READING Dev Patel

This text is from an online British movie magazine. Read the whole article through first, then do the two tasks on the next page.

Meet Dev Patel, teenage movie star

The hit movie *Slumdog Millionaire* tells the story of 17-year-old Jamal, one of the millions of extremely poor people (the 'slumdogs') who live in the slums[1] of India's largest city, Mumbai. Jamal goes on the Indian TV gameshow *Who Wants to Be a Millionaire?*, answers all the questions correctly, wins the top prize – and finds the girl he loves. In 2009, the movie won eight Oscars. Its star was the young English actor Dev Patel …

When Dev Patel arrived in Mumbai to film *Slumdog Millionaire*, it was only his second visit to India. In fact, learning the Mumbai accent was, he says, one of the hardest things he had to do. He wasn't a famous actor, either. He had liked drama very much at school in England, and he had played a small part in a British TV series, but that was all. So how did he become Jamal and what was it like when he was suddenly an international movie star?

Dev was born near London in 1993. His parents are Indians who had moved to England when they were young. His dad is a computer technician, his mum a carer[2].

Dev went to a 'typical' English secondary school. His first hobby was martial arts – karate then tae kwon do. He was excellent at both and even took part in the Youth Olympics. But after a role in a school play, Dev found that what he really loved was acting.

His mum wanted to encourage him, and when Dev was 14, she showed him a small advertisement in a newspaper. A TV company wanted people for a series called Skins, about a group of teenage friends. Dev wrote a reply – and got a part.

Three years later – Dev was 17 – the successful British film director Danny Boyle was looking for someone to play Jamal in *Slumdog Millionaire*.

Mumbai is the home of the huge Indian movie industry. People sometimes call it Bollywood: Bombay (the old name for Mumbai) plus Hollywood. The problem was that young, male Bollywood actors are all very strong and handsome. Boyle wanted a young man who looked more like a 'slumdog'. It was Boyle's daughter who told her dad about Dev – she often watched Skins. Dev had five auditions[3] ('I was crying at the end because I didn't think I'd get the part', he says) but then he was Jamal.

For Dev, the next five months were like a dream. He was in Mumbai and on a movie set. With him were a world-famous director, some of the best known older Bollywood stars, real kids from the slums of Mumbai, and the beautiful young actress who is his girlfriend in the movie. 'I grew up five years in those five months,' Dev says.

What did the real people from Mumbai's slums think? Dev was amazed by them. They were so proud that they were in the movie. 'Don't tell people we're poor,' they said to Dev and Boyle. 'Tell them we're happy. We aren't poor because we're happy.'

[1] slum [slʌm] *Slum, Elendsviertel* [2] carer ['keərə] *(Alten-)Pfleger/in* [3] audition [ɔː'dɪʃn] *Sprechprobe*

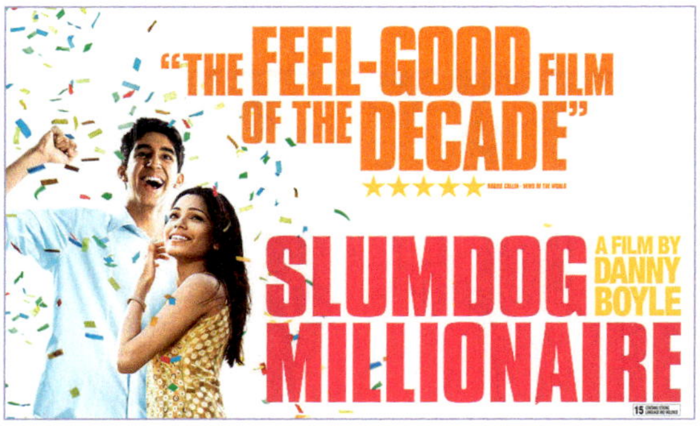

Questions on the text

a) *Choose the correct answer – A, B, C or D.*

1 What do you learn most about in this article?
A the Indian movie industry.
B the film *Slumdog Millionaire*.
C the young English actor Dev Patel.
D the life of the poor people in the slums of Mumbai.

2 The article says Dev Patel got the lead role in *Slumdog Millionaire* because ....
A he was strong and handsome.
B he knew Danny Boyle's daughter.
C he really loved acting.
D he looked a bit like a 'slumdog'.

3 In the movie, Dev plays the role of a young Indian man who ...
A wins an Oscar.
B becomes a millionaire.
C moves to Mumbai.
D tells a story.

4 Before he acted in the film *Slumdog Millionaire*, Dev ...
A was already a famous actor.
B had lived for a long time in Mumbai.
C had only played a small role in a TV series.
D could speak with a Mumbai accent.

5 Dev ...
A has Indian parents but grew up in England.
B has English parents and grew up in England.
C has Indian parents and moved to England when he was small.
D has English parents but grew up in India.

6 Which activity interested Dev most when he was at school?
A tae kwon do
B acting
C the Youth Olympics
D karate

7 How did Dev get the part in Skins?
A His dad helped him.
B A TV company wrote to him.
C He often watched it on TV.
D He replied to a newspaper advertisement.

b) *Finish the sentences with information from the text.*

8 Danny Boyle, the director of *Slumdog Millionaire*, chose Dev for the part of Jamal and not a young, male Bollywood actor because Dev ...
9 Mr Boyle found out about Dev from ...
10 At the end of his auditions, Dev was crying because ...
11 Filming *Slumdog Millionaire* in Mumbai changed Dev a lot. He describes this change when he tells us that ...
12 Dev expected the people who lived in the slums of Mumbai to be really sad. In fact, he found that although they are poor, ...

4 SPEAKING Talking about a picture

Partner A

Describe to your partner what you can see in the photo on the right.
(Partner B: just listen).
Speak for around one minute.
- *Who are the people in the photo? Where are they? What are they doing?*
- *Describe their feelings.*
- *Would you like to be one of the people in the photo? Why (not)?*

Partner B

Now it's your turn. Describe to your partner what you can see in the photo on the right.
(Partner A: just listen).
Speak for around one minute.
- *Who are the people in the photo? Where are they? What are they doing?*
- *Describe their feelings.*
- *Would you like to be one of the people in the photo? Why (not)?*

5 SPEAKING Hobbies and interests

Now talk to your partner. Tell each other about your hobbies and interests.
Talk together for about three minutes. Here are some ideas:

- What do you like doing in your free time? Why?
- Where, when and how often do you do those things?
- Do you do them alone, with your family or with friends?
- Describe the last time you did one of the activities.
- Is there one thing that you hate doing?

How am I doing?

Check your answers to tasks 1 and 3 in the Answer key.

About the test

This second test gave you the chance again to try some of the kinds of tasks that you will do one day in your exam (*Abschlussprüfung*). This time, the tasks tested your reading, mediation and speaking skills. If you found some tasks difficult, don't worry. You've got lots of time to practise. Remember: 'Practice makes perfect!'

Reading

Task 1 and task 3 in the test were reading tasks. The following three questions will help you to think about how you did. Read the questions and tick the boxes that are right for you.

1 **How hard or easy was each task?**

	easy	OK	quite hard	very hard
Task 1	❑	❑	❑	❑
Task 2	❑	❑	❑	❑
Task 3	❑	❑	❑	❑

2 **What was difficult in the tasks?**

- The texts were quite long and complicated. ❑
- There were words and phrases that I just couldn't understand. ❑
- There was a lot of information. I couldn't find the exact answers. ❑
- The tasks weren't like the tasks that we do in class. ❑

3 **How did you do the tasks?**

- I always read the questions carefully so that I knew what to look for in the texts. ❑
- I tried to understand the main ideas of the text first. That helped me to guess words that I wasn't sure about. ❑
- If there was a question that I wasn't sure about, I left it out and came back to it later. ❑
- I scanned the text when I looked for a special piece of information. ❑
- I checked my answers at the end to make sure I hadn't made a 'silly' mistake. ❑

Speaking

1 Copy and fill in the assessment sheet below about your partner's description in the fourth task (Talking about a picture).

Assessment sheet				
Name of partner ...	☺	😐	☹	Comments
Did your partner ...				
1 ... speak clearly and loudly enough?				
2 ... find enough to say?				
3 ... answer all the questions?				
4 ... have problems finding the right words?				
5 ... make grammar or vocabulary mistakes?				

2 Now look at the checklist on the right and talk about how well you did in the fifth task, the dialogue about your hobbies and interests.

- We listened to each other. ❑
- We only gave short answers. ❑
- We showed interest in each other. ❑
- There was a good flow in our dialogue.[1] ❑

[1] There was a good flow in our dialogue. *Unser Gespräch verlief flüssig.*

Getting ready for a test 1

1 LISTENING Travelling to Australia

1 A Gate 17
2 C chicken with salad or pasta
3 A just over there
4 B $ 52.50
5 C 07:00–10:30

2 LISTENING Shark attack

a)
1 C New South Wales
2 A surfing
3 D leg
4 B 5 seconds
5 C Jon swam back to the beach
6 C scariest

b)
1 ... they **tied** a rope round his **leg** ...
2 ... but he **didn't lose his leg** / **survived** / **is alive**.
3 ... **attack** / **kill** people.
4 ... in Australia every **day** than from shark attacks **in ten years.**
5 ... always swim **in groups**, so your friends can help you. And never swim **in the early morning or in the evening** ...

3 LISTENING Young Australians and the internet

1 False
2 True
3 False
4 True
5 True
6 True

4 WRITING An online magazine for young Europeans

(individuelle Lösungen)

Getting ready for a test 2

1 READING Choosing a book

1 Student A – Book 7
2 Student B – Book 5
3 Student C – Book 3
4 Student D – Book 1
5 Student E – Book 4

2 MEDIATION A note to your friend

(individuelle Lösungen)

3 READING Dev Patel

a)
1 C the young English actor Dev Patel
2 C quite surprising that
3 B becomes a millionaire.
4 C had only played a small role in a TV series.
5 A has Indian parents but grew up in England.
6 B acting
7 D He replied to a newspaper advertisement.

b)
8 ... looked more like a 'slumdog'
9 ... his daughter.
10 ... he didn't think he'd get the part.
11 ... he grew up five years in five months.
12 ... they are happy.

4 SPEAKING Talking about a picture

(individuelle Lösungen)

5 SPEAKING Hobbies and interests

(individuelle Lösungen)

A TEXT-BASED TASKS *22 pts*

1

Match the two halves of the sentences. *5 pts*

1	A politician and some students	A	are still there.
2	The problems Senator Nelson saw almost 50 years ago	B	a big international meeting.
3	Today there is more pollution	C	organized the first Earth Day.
4	Earth Day is	D	than in 1962.
5	The first Earth Day brought together	E	millions of people.

1 ☐ 2 ☐ 3 ☐ 4 ☐ 5 ☐

2

Find the information from the text. Write complete sentences. *11 pts*

1. What is the purpose of Earth Day? (1 item)

___

2. What different kinds of pollution did Senator Nelson see? (3 items)

___

3. What do environmental organizations help people do? (4 items)

___

4. How can school-children fight against pollution? (3 items)

___

3

Ask questions. *6 pts*

A friend calls you on your mobile phone. He is in the street, taking part in a local Earth Day march in your town and he asks you to join him. You want to get some more information.
*Ask him **four** questions. Use at least **three** different question forms.*

1 ___

2 ___

3 ___

4 ___

B Use of Language 19 pts

1 *Vocabulary – Grammar*

Read the text. Find suitable forms of the words and write them down. 12 pts

The North Yorkshire Moors in England is one of the (1.) ______________________ parts of Britain. It is a (2.) ______________________ beautiful region and many people come here for a walking or hiking holiday because it is so (3.) ______________________ and (4.) ______________________. The scenery is (5.) ______________________ and you can see wildlife such as deer and eagles. There is a big choice of (6.) ______________________ activities to do such as hang gliding, rock climbing and pony trekking. For walkers, it is important to wear strong walking shoes because the ground can be (7.) ______________________.

The Moors cover a very big area and you can spend all day walking without seeing anyone. So a compass and a map are very (8.) ______________________ in case you get (9.) ______________________ ! Throughout the Moors there are small (10.) ______________________ villages with simple but (11.) ______________________ inns and hostels where hikers can stay overnight and have a big healthy breakfast before (12.) ______________________ again.

1.	wild	4.	relax	7.	rock	10.	tradition
2.	particular	5.	impress	8.	use	11.	comfort
3.	peace	6.	excite	9.	lose	12.	set off

2

Write complete sentences to explain the meaning of ***two*** *of the following words.* 4 pts

1. celebration (line 7) ______________________
2. rubbish (line 12) ______________________
3. environment (line 17) ______________________

3

Find the words in the text that have more or less the same meaning. 3 pts

1. aim (lines 1–8) ______________________
2. during (lines 27–37) ______________________
3. take part (lines 38–52) ______________________

C Creative Writing 27 pts

1 ***What would you do or say?*** *9 pts*
Choose **two** *of the situations and explain yourself. Write 60 words altogether.*

a) During a lesson about the environment, your teacher asks you to suggest ways to help reduce wasting water and paper.

b) In your local shop, you see a girl take a packet of chewing gum and put it in her pocket without paying.

c) You live in a town on the coast. A tanker at sea has spilt oil and it has reached the town beach.

2 *Choose task A* **or** *B. Write about 120 words altogether.* *18 pts*

A *Write an article.*

You are part of a school committee of pupils . Your task is to go round your school building and playground to inspect them for damage and rubbish. Write about what you did and what you found for the school magazine.

B *Write a story.*

Start like this:
The noise got louder and louder. So I got up and went over to the window, opened the curtains and looked out. I saw the strangest thing!

D Skills and Techniques 22 pts

1 *Mediation* 10 pts

Ein britischer Umweltexperte hat an deiner Schule einen Vortrag zum Thema „Dein Beitrag gegen die Verschmutzung“ gehalten. Was wurde über die unten stehenden Fragen ausgesagt?

You may think that you can't do much to help protect the environment. That it is too complicated and you need a lot of money. And maybe you feel that young people aren't really concerned. After all, it is adults who drive cars, work in factories, buy petrol and cut down trees. But you are wrong. It is young people like you who can do an enormous amount to protect the environment by simply talking about it and being environment-friendly yourselves! There are lots of small ways you can help directly. If you start now, hopefully you will continue the good habits as you get older. And it won't cost you a cent! For example, you can reduce the amount of traffic fumes simply by walking or cycling and not relying on parents to give you a lift. And when you get a car of your own, organize car-sharing with your friends and neighbours. One car with four people in it is better than four cars with one person in each of them! Persuade your Mum not to use the car all the time for shopping, to get it all done in one trip and walk to local shops more often. And, talking of shopping, don't use plastic bags to bring it all home! Imagine the millions of bags being manufactured in factories – factories which contribute to air pollution and bags which take years to disappear. It is much better – and just as easy – to take your own shopping basket! And, by the way, check the labels on the things you buy and reduce chemical products to the minimum.

I am sure you can think of lots of ways in your everyday life at home and at school to protect the environment: reducing pollution, saving precious water, and respecting the countryside and wild animals. It is essential to maintain the delicate balance of nature because, without that balance, the environment will be destroyed. And, don't forget, we human beings are part of that environment! *(332 words)*

Fragen

1. Wie können junge Leute die Erwachsenen in ihrem Umweltverhalten beeinflussen? (2 Punkte)
2. Kannst du zwei Beispiele geben, wie man Verkehrsabgase reduzieren kann? (2 Punkte)
3. Warum ist es besser, keine Plastiktüten zu verwenden? (2 Punkte)
4. Wie können wir sicherstellen, dass die von uns gekauften Produkte umweltverträglich sind? (2 Punkte)
5. Warum ist die Natur für uns Menschen so wichtig? (2 Punkte)

2 *Translate the following paragraph into German.* **12** *pts*

Imagine a day when 500 million people from 184 countries around the world come together to celebrate and protest with a single purpose in mind. This is just what happened on April 22nd, 2000. The day was Earth Day, and the purpose that the people had in mind was to work for a healthier and safer world for everyone. It was the biggest celebration of its kind in human history.

5 Sailing Teens

When Seb Clover was just twelve years old, he already knew more about sailing than most adults. His father, Ian, who is a sailing instructor at the Isle of Wight UK Sailing Academy, had taught him all about yachts and sailboats.

One day, Seb's mum said to him and his father, "You two are so competitive! Why don't you have a race to see who is the best yachtsman?" She was only joking, but Seb and Ian took the idea very seriously. For the next three years Seb spent every free moment training with his dad, and on December 19th, 2002, Seb set sail from Tenerife, Spain, on the greatest adventure of his life: a race across the Atlantic Ocean against his father.

Seb and Ian sailed alone aboard identical 9.8-metre Contessa yachts, so that neither would have an advantage. It took them three weeks to reach English Harbour, Antigua. In the end, Seb lost the race but, at the age of 15, he became the youngest person ever to cross the Atlantic on a solo voyage.

"The highlights were definitely seeing whales and dolphins... and especially reaching Antigua," says Seb. The worst moment was when he ran out of chocolate half-way through the 4,345-kilometre voyage.

Of course, not everyone can enter the record books like Seb Clover. But every day there are more and more ways for teens to enjoy sailing. Student Ben East took part in the Round Britain Challenge 2006, a non-stop race round Britain and Ireland. "Life was at the best of times 'interesting' and, at the worst, almost impossible," says Ben, who spent twelve days on a 22-metre yacht with 17 other amateur yachts-men and two professional seamen. Ben was the youngest crew member, and says of the experience, "It gave me the confidence to express my thoughts and be counted as a team member."

Another option for teens is sailing camp. For around 4,000 Euros, companies like Quest Voyages and Oddysey Expeditions offer teens between the ages of 13 and 19 the chance to earn sailing and scuba diving certificates while exploring the waters and islands of the Mediterranean, the Caribbean or Australia. Giorgina de Limon from Brussels says of her three-week-long adventure: "The best parts of the programme were the diving and sailing. The instructors were really good and the equipment was the best you could get." Catherine Leahy from Toulouse explains: "I learnt so much during those three weeks, from scuba diving to sailing to living with others. It was a fantastic trip."

It is no wonder then that yacht clubs around the world report that their members are getting younger and younger. Every day there are more sailing teens like Seb, Ben, Giorgina and Catherine. *(452 words)*

A TEXT-BASED TASKS *17 pts*

1 *Correct the following statements.* *5 pts*
You need not write the complete sentence again – just correct the false words or phrases.

1. Ian's father is a swimming instructor. ______
2. Seb spent very little time training for the race against his father. ______
3. The boats that Seb and his father sailed were very different. ______
4. Seb and his Dad sailed from the Isle of Wight to Antigua. ______
5. It was Seb who won the race. ______

2 ***Who is who?*** *6 pts*
There are four teenagers mentioned in the text (Seb, Ben, Giorgina and Catherine).
Write down the name of the person described in these sentences.

1. ______ went sailing with seamen who were all older.
2. ______ crossed the Atlantic single-handed.
3. ______ found the equipment very good.
4. ______ learnt a lot of things on a three-week sailing trip.
5. ______ sailed around the British Isles.
6. ______ was impressed by the instructors.

3 ***Ask questions.*** *6 pts*
You're interviewing Seb about his race across the Atlantic Ocean. Write ***four*** *questions to ask him.*
Use at least ***three*** *different question forms.*

1 ______

2 ______

3 ______

4 ______

B Use of Language 20 pts

1 *Vocabulary – Grammar*

Read the text. Find suitable forms of the words and write them down. 14 pts

Many (1.) ____________ baseball players in the United States come from the small Caribbean state of the Dominican Republic. In the late 19th century, there was a wave of (2.) ____________ to the island from Cuba. People came to work in the sugar mills and (3.) ____________ the game with them. Now the (4.) ____________ of the sugar industry means that baseball is all that is (5.) ____________. The main centre is San Pedro de Macoris. (6.) ____________ kids come from miles around looking for a (7.) ____________ to train. There is a lot of (8.) ____________ in the Dominican Republic so it is (9.) ____________ that it is everyone's dream to have a baseball player in the family. It is a sport that can make a great (10.) ____________ to the lives of ordinary Dominicans. Some of the kids show (11.) ____________ talent and find (12.) ____________ as star players in US leagues. It is no (13.) ____________ to say that the US depends on the small island for its (14.) ____________ sport.

1.	profession	5.	leave	9.	understand	13.	exaggerate
2.	emigrate	6.	hope	10.	different	14.	nation
3.	bring	7.	possible	11.	amaze		
4.	disappear	8.	poor	12.	successful		

2

Find words or phrases in the text which have more or less the same meaning. 6 pts

1. to start a journey at sea (lines 6–14) ____________
2. on a boat (lines 15–20) ____________
3. a long journey alone across the ocean (lines 15–20) ____________
4. to say what you think (lines 26–37) ____________
5. the opportunity (lines 38–45) ____________
6. It is not surprising. (lines 48–55) ____________

C Creative Writing *27 pts*

1 *Give your opinion on* **two** *of the following statements. Write about 60 words altogether.* *9 pts*

a) Sailing is a sport for rich people.

b) Sailing is not really a sport – it is just a leisure activity.

c) Sport is too dangerous – there are other ways to stay healthy.

2 *Choose task A* ***or*** *B. Write about 120 words altogether.* *18 pts*

A *Write a letter.*

You've just come back from a holiday camp for young people at the seaside. Write a letter to your British friend and tell him about the activities there.

B *Write a story about a dangerous situation at sea. Use the following expressions in your text.*

yacht terrible storm rescue

D Skills and Techniques 26 pts

1 *Mediation* 14 *pts*

Unten stehend findest du einen Artikel über die bekannte britische Seglerin Ellen MacArthur. Dein Freund, der kein Englisch versteht, hat einige Fragen zu Ellens Biografie, die du auf Deutsch beantworten sollst.

Imagine spending months alone on the ocean, sleeping in 20-minute intervals and lifting equipment far heavier than you are. This is the life and passion of the British yachtswoman, Ellen MacArthur. Ellen won the famous Vendée Globe Race in 2004 and became the fastest woman sailor and the youngest Briton to sail around the world non-stop.

How did Ellen become a champion? Ironically she grew up in the middle of England a long way from the sea. Her passion for sailing began when her aunt took her on a boat trip when she was 8. From that moment on, she was hooked! She read every sailing book she could find and took part in local sailing club races. By saving up her pocket money for 3 years and with help from her Granny, she bought her first boat. At 18, she sailed single-handedly around Britain and won the Young Sailor of the Year Award. She then started to take part in international races, improving her performance each time and was awarded the title Yachtsman of the Year.

But her major achievement was the Vendée Globe Race. Many people believed she was too young at 25, and too small at only 1.55m in height. Would she have the strength to sail alone for three months, make repairs, sail through storms, avoid icebergs, fight extreme tiredness and, all the while, keep sailing on course? Well, she did. And when she sailed through the finishing line in Britanny, Northern France, there were 20,000 people waiting to greet her.

"I'm lucky to be doing what I love", she says. She believes in sharing her luck. In her cabin there is a photo of a little girl smiling. She is one of a group of children with cancer whom Ellen takes on sailing trips. "Those kids have big problems but they keep smiling", she says. "When I'm at sea facing problems, I think of those smiles and it keeps me going". *(325 words)*

12 to be hooked *sich für etwas begeistern, Feuer und Flamme sein.*

Fragen

1. Wofür ist Ellen MacArthur berühmt? (2 Fakten) (2 Punkte)
2. Warum ist es überraschend, dass Ellen zum Segelsport kam? (2 Punkte)
3. Wie hat Ellens Leidenschaft für das Segeln angefangen? (2 Punkte)
4. Wie konnte sie sich ihr erstes Boot leisten? (2 Punkte)
5. Welche Herausforderungen musste sie sich während des Vendée-Globe-Rennens stellen? (2 Punkte)
6. Welche Preise hat Ellen noch gewonnen? (2 Punkte)
7. Auf welche Weise lässt Ellen andere Menschen an ihrer Leidenschaft für den Segelsport teilhaben? (2 Punkte)

2 *Translate the following paragraph into German.* **12** *pts*

"You two are so competitive! Why don't you have a race to see who is the best yachtsman?" His mother was only joking, but Seb and his dad took the idea very seriously. For the next three years Seb spent every free moment training with his dad, and on December 19th, 2002, Seb set sail from Tenerife, Spain, on the greatest adventure of his life: a race across the Atlantic Ocean against his father.

6 One Who Understands

When Matt Kelley was growing up in the United States, he often thought to himself, "Who am I?". Of course, there is nothing unusual about this; most teenagers ask themselves the same question from time to time. But Matt's problem was special. When he saw his schoolmates, he didn't see anyone who looked like him. There were white kids and black kids, Asian kids and Hispanic kids, but none like him. And when Matt went home and switched on the TV or opened a magazine, he still didn't see anyone who was quite like him.

Matt Kelley was a multiracial teen: his dad was white and his mum was Korean. He felt that he didn't quite fit in with white kids because of his Asian side, and that he didn't quite fit in with Asians because he was half white. This made him feel confused and frustrated, and he often wondered if he was the only teenager in the world with this problem.

In Matt's first year at university, he met other multiracial young people, and he began to talk with them about the problems that they had in common. He soon realized that there were lots of multiracial people in the U.S. and that they didn't really have a place to discuss their experiences. So when Matt was only 19, he founded MAVIN. MAVIN means "one who understands" in Hebrew[1]. It is a magazine for young multiracial people who want to read about other people of mixed race and their experiences. It publishes articles about the unique problems that affect multiracial teens and invites its readers to write their own stories for publication in the magazine.

In a recent survey, when a group of American teens were asked if they had ever dated someone of a different race or ethnic background, 60% said yes. This, and the popularity of multiracial celebrities[2] like Tiger Woods, Halle Berry, Lenny Kravitz and Mariah Carey, has made people reconsider the old concepts of race. "Multiracial means disregarding old models," explains Matt Kelley. "It means there are no boundaries to race. We can be comfortable being whatever we want to be."

Today, in addition to editing his magazine, Matt is president of the MAVIN Foundation, an organization that gives support to multiracial teens and their families. He is truly "one who understands".

(392 words)

1 ***Hebrew*** *Hebräisch*
2 ***celebrities*** *Berühmtheiten*

A TEXT-BASED TASKS 17 pts

1 *Finish these sentences using information from the text.* 5 pts

1. Matt's problem was that ______
2. Matt discovered that there were a lot of multiracial people when ______
3. Matt's magazine MAVIN is for ______
4. The magazine articles are about ______
5. The MAVIN Foundation is an organization which ______

2 *Find the information in the text. Write complete sentences.* 6 pts

1. What kind of kids did he go to school with? ______
2. Why is Matt described as multiracial? ______
3. What are MAVIN readers encouraged to do? ______

3 ***Ask questions.*** 6 pts

A survey

An English friend is doing a survey of the multiracial students in his school. He is writing a questionnaire. Suggest some questions that he could ask the students. Write ***four*** *questions. Use at least* ***three*** *different question forms.*

1 ______

2 ______

3 ______

4 ______

B USE OF LANGUAGE 20 pts

1 *Vocabulary – Grammar*

Read the text. Find suitable forms of the words and write them down. 14 pts

What is life (1.) ____________ like for kids today? If you look at the media, it seems as if the world is a (2.) ____________ place. There is (3.) ____________ everywhere, and (4.) ____________ and (5.) ____________ in schools and on the streets. Environmental (6.) ____________ could mean the (7.) ____________ of our planet. Our kids lead (8.) ____________ lives. They eat junk food and spend all their free-time (9.) ____________ computer games. There are no jobs and a lot of them will be (10.) ____________ when they leave school. Happily, a survey (11.) ____________ that young people have a more positive (12.) ____________ of the world . They enjoy more (13.) ____________ than the generations before them. Their free-time is full of interesting (14.) ____________ and many of them want to make the world a better place.

1.	real	5.	vandal	9.	play	13.	free
2.	depressed	6.	pollute	10.	employ	14.	active
3.	dangerous	7.	destroy	11.	show		
4.	violent	8.	health	12.	impress		

2

Find the word or words in the text that have more or less the same meaning. 6 pts

1. young people between 13 and 19 years of age (lines 1–11) ____________
2. puzzled (lines 12–18) ____________
3. he found out (lines 19–32) ____________
4. he created (lines 19–32) ____________
5. went out with (lines 33–42) ____________
6. well-known stars in entertainment and sport (lines 33–42) ____________

C Creative Writing *27 pts*

1 *What would you do or say?* *9 pts*

Choose **two** *of the following situations and explain yourself. Write about 60 words altogether.*

a) You're buying a ticket at the cinema and realize you have forgotten your student card which gives you a 50% reduction.

b) There's a new Asian pupil in your class. She's finding it difficult to understand the lesson.

c) You see a classmate bullying a pupil at your school.

____

____

____

____

____

____

____

2 *Choose task A* **or** *B. Write about 120 words altogether.* *18 pts*

A *Write a story.*

Here is a sentence from the **middle** of a story. Write the beginning and the end of the story:
'Just then, the head teacher walked in. I was so embarrassed.'

B *Write a letter.*

Write a letter to your American penfriend to tell him / her about World Day – a multiracial day held in your school last week. Each class organized a different activity which included:

- cooking food from different countries
- playing music from around the world
- presenting clothes from different countries

D Skills and Techniques 26 pts

1 *Mediation* 14 pts

Im folgenden Text geht es um die Vor- und Nachteile der Vielvölkergesellschaften. Deine Freundin interessiert sich für den Text, aber ihr Englisch ist nicht so gut. Sie hat die unten stehenden Fragen gestellt. Bitte beantworte sie auf Deutsch.

Multiracialism

Multiracialism means a mixture of people with different backgrounds, languages, cultures, religions and traditions.

Countries such as the United States, the United Kingdom and Singapore are good examples of multiracial societies.

In 2000 it was estimated that 75.1% of the population of the United States were white, mostly of European origin, 12.5 % were Hispanics, 12.3 % blacks or African Americans; 3.7% Asians and Pacific Islanders, and 0.9 % Native Americans.

In Singapore – often said to be one of the most politically stable countries in the world – there are four main ethnic groups: Chinese, Indian, Malay and Eurasian. English serves as a link between the different ethnic groups and is the language of education and administration.

Beginning with the post-war immigration boom, the United Kingdom has gradually developed into a multiracial society. The three largest groups with immigrant backgrounds are from India, Pakistan and the Caribbean.

Living in a multiracial society has many advantages. Such societies can be very lively and colourful. People in these societes have a chance to learn about other cultures, traditions and food, and to take over the positive aspects for themselves. There may also be more opportunities to learn other languages. In a multiracial society we can learn to understand and respect other cultures and religions and become more tolerant.

As a result of people from different cultures intermarrying, there are now many children with a multiracial background. This has advantages and disadvantages. In many families the children are taught to see their different backgrounds and languages as equally important. These children grow up with a more open view of the world, and they easily accept different cultures and languages.

One disadvantage of a multiracial background is that a child may be confused about his or her own identity. Multiracial people may also find it difficult to decide whether to identify themselves with their father's or mother's racial group or both. Some children may simply feel "American" or "English" and not identify with their parents' backgrounds at all.

In a world of globalization, where moving from one country to another and intermarrying are becoming more and more common, it is only a matter of time before a multiracial society is the norm. *(368 words)*

Fragen

1. Was bedeutet „multiracialism"? (2 Punkte)
2. Welche ist die größte und welche die kleinste ethnische Gruppe in den USA? (1 Punkt)
3. Was verbindet die vier ethnischen Gruppen in Singapur? (1 Punkt)
4. Menschen mit Migrationshintergrund im Vereinigten Königreich kommen aus verschiedenen Ländern. Nenne zwei davon. (2 Punkte)
5. Welche Vorteile hat man, wenn man in einem Vielvölkergesellschaft lebt? (2 Fakten) (2 Punkte)
6. Welche Vorteile gibt es für Kinder, deren Eltern aus verschiedenen Kulturen stammen? (2 Fakten) (2 Punkte)
7. Welche Nachteile haben Kinder, deren Eltern aus verschiedenen Kulturen stammen? (2 Fakten) (2 Punkte)
8. Warum könnte eine Vielvölkergesellschaft zur Norm werden? (2 Punkte)

2 *Translate the following paragraph into German.* **12** *pts*

When Matt Kelley was growing up in the United States, he often thought to himself, "Who am I?". Of course, there is nothing unusual about this; most teenagers ask themselves the same question from time to time. But Matt's problem was special. When he saw his schoolmates, he didn't see anyone who looked like him. There were white kids and black kids, Asian kids and Hispanic kids*, but none like him.

___

___

___

___

___

___

___

___

___

* ***Hispanic kids*** *Braucht nicht übersetzt zu werden.*

7 Australian Connection

After passing his exams 18-year-old Alex decided to travel to Australia to visit his father, Tom, who he hadn't seen since his parents were divorced fifteen years ago.
To get to know each other, father and son went on a trip to Queensland. On their way they had to stop at a river that crossed the road. A sign said:

DANGER – CROCODILES!

Fortunately, Tom was not eaten by a crocodile. Even more fortunately, at its deepest, the water only came up to Tom's knees, and the four-wheel drive crossed the river with no problems. Two hours later they arrived at a hostel, deep within the rain forest at the foot of Mount Sorrow.

The next couple of days went far too quickly for Alex. He and Tom went walking through the steaming rain forest; they followed the boardwalk through the mangrove swamp; they rode horses along the sandy beach; they visited a crocodile reserve. Alex found himself surrounded by birds and insects, trees and flowers that he had only ever seen before on television.

"It's fantastic!" Alex said again and again, as he saw more and more wonderful sights. "Really fantastic!"

"I'm glad you like it," said Tom. "I love it here. The trouble is, it's all changing. People from the cities are buying up the land and building holiday homes. Slowly but surely, the forest is being destroyed."

Alex looked at Tom. The trip had been wonderful so far. And yet it was not how Alex had imagined it would be. He felt somehow that he had lost a father, but found a friend.

After a final walk – to the top of Mount Sorrow – Tom and Alex packed up the four-wheel drive and left. By midday, they were back at the river which had been so full and fast before. Now, it was just a shallow stream and Tom drove across easily.

Alex turned and looked back through the rear-window at the rain forest. Beautiful and remote, it had remained untouched for thousands of years. Now all that had changed, and if strict laws were not soon made, the rain forest and everything in it would disappear for ever.

"It's so sad," he said.

Tom nodded. "People can be very, very stupid," he agreed angrily.

As they left the rain forest behind and the roads improved, Tom began to cheer up. He told Alex all about Gypsy Woman, the boat he shared with his brother, which was moored[1] in Cairns.

"I thought we'd take her out onto the reef," he said.

"The Great Barrier Reef?" Alex asked excitedly.

"That's the one," Tom smiled.

Alex grinned. He knew all about the Great Barrier Reef, of course. He had learnt about it in geography lessons and had always wanted to see the multi-coloured coral for himself. Now he was going to do just that.

"Is it as wonderful as it looks on film?" he asked.

"Better," Tom answered. "A million times better."

(493 words)

1 **moored** *vor Anker lag*

A Text-based Tasks 20 pts

1

After you have read the text, read the following extract from the diary that Alex kept during his Australian trip. 13 of the facts are wrong. Underline the incorrect words and write down the correct facts at the end of the line. The first one is done for you. 6 pts

"The water came above Tom's knees so we could walk across the river easily (1.) up to (2.) ______

It took us all afternoon to reach the hostel at the top of Mount Sorrow. (3.) ______ (4.) ______

The next seven days were fantastic. We rode horses through the rain forest; (5.) ______ (6.) ______

we walked along the beach, and we visited a crocodile reserve. Everywhere (7.) ______

I went I saw amazing insects, birds, flowers and trees I had only read about (8.) ______

before. On the final day we walked down Mount Sorrow and arrived back at (9.) ______

the river by the evening. It was strange how the river, so shallow on our first (10.) ______ (11.) ______

day, was now very full and we only just managed to drive across. Tom has (12.) ______ (13.) ______
promised to take me to the Great Barrier Reef. I'm really looking forward to seeing it!

2

A reporter is asking Tom questions about the rain forest. 8 pts
Write down Tom's answers in complete sentences. The answers are not necessarily in the text.

1. Why do a lot of city people buy up land in the rain forest?

______

2. How can they be stopped from doing this?

______

3. What will happen if they continue?

______

4. What's your opinion of people who do this?

______

3

Ask questions. 6 pts

Alex is phoning his mother back in the UK. Write down ***two*** *questions she asks Alex about his trip and* ***two*** *questions about his relationship with his father, Tom. Use at least* ***three*** *different question forms.*

1 ______

2 ______

3 ______

4 ______

B Use of Language 19 pts

1

*Find the **opposite** of these words and phrases in the text.* 5 pts

1. awful (line 15–24) ______
2. hate (line 15–24) ______
3. cheerfully (lines 35–42) ______
4. got worse (lines 35–42) ______
5. to be depressed (lines 35–42) ______

2

Vocabulary – Grammar
Read the text. Find the suitable forms of the words and write them down. 11 pts

Welcome to Australia's Great Barrier Reef!

The Great Barrier Reef has captured man's (1.) ______ ever since it was discovered in the 17th and 18th century by European (2.) ______. It is situated off the north east coast of Australia and is over 2,000 kilometres in (3.) ______. It is composed of hundreds of different types of coral and is home to an incredible (4.) ______ of sea plants and animals. Sailing and scuba –diving in the GBR is a (5.) ______ experience! Sail from Cairns over to one of the reef islands and watch (6.) ______ whales and (7.) ______ dolphins swimming alongside the boat! Plunge into the clear turquoise water and swim along with shoals of (8.) ______ coloured fish! Walk along the long white (9.) ______ beaches looking for shells and coral. The Great Barrier Reef has taken thousands of years to evolve but is a very fragile environment. This is why it is protected by the Australian Government who (10.) ______ that it is used in the least harmful but the most enjoyable way by the large numbers of (11.) ______ who visit the area every year.

1.	imagine	4.	vary	7.	play	10.	sure
2.	explore	5.	memory	8.	bright	11.	tour
3.	long	6.	friend	9.	sand		

3 *Prepositions* *3 pts*

Complete the sentences with the prepositions listed below.

1. He dived into the cold water and swam ________________ the river.
2. I saw her come ________________ the cinema while I was waiting in the queue.
3. The local people are fed up with heavy lorries driving ________________ their village!
4. "The station? You go ________________ this road and it's on the left."
5. I cycled ________________ the bridge as fast as I could.
6. As the boat sailed into shore, he jumped out ________________ the sand.

through	across	onto	over	along	out of

C Creative Writing 27 *pts*

1 *What advice would you give to someone going on the same trip to the rain forest as Alex?* 9 *pts*
Write about 60 words altogether.

2 *Choose task A **or** B. Write about 120 words altogether.* 18 *pts*

A *Write an email.*

This is part of an email you have received from Jack, an Australian relative you are going to visit:

> ... I'm really looking forward to your visit. What shall we plan to do? Write and tell me soon ...

Write back to Jack and tell him the things you are interested in doing.

B *Write a letter.*

Imagine you are Alex. Write a letter to your Dad thanking him for the holiday you spent with him. Talk about the things you did, the moments you liked best and your feelings for him.

D Skills and Techniques 24 pts

1 *Mediation* 12 pts

Auf einer Kundgebung in England hast du ein Flugblatt mit dem Titel RAIN FORESTS IN DANGER erhalten. Dein Freund zu Hause interessiert sich für das Thema und schickt eine E-Mail mit den unten stehenden Fragen

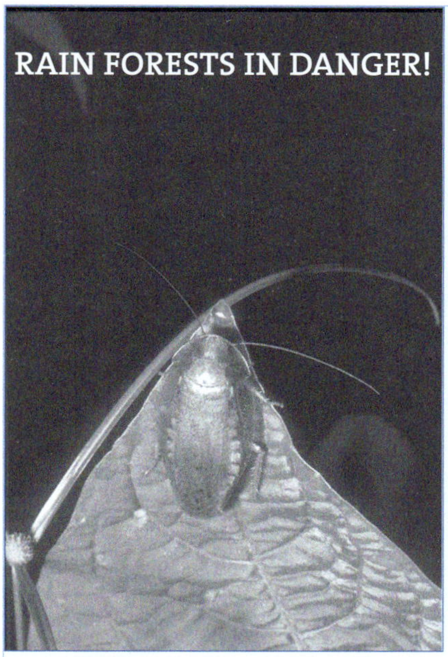

The Amazon rain forest is being destroyed! Stop this destruction! We need rain forests! Look at these important facts:

- The Amazon rain forest produces 20% of the oxygen that we breathe on this earth!
- The plants in the forest change carbon dioxide into clean air. This helps fight pollution and prevents the earth warming up – the greenhouse effect.
- The Amazon rain forest contains an enormous diversity of plants and animals – many of which are found nowhere else on earth!
- The Amazon rain forest and surrounding regions contain 30% of the world's fresh water!
- The Amazon rain forest has plants that are used in medicine. 60% of The drugs which fight cancer and other deadly diseases come from plants that can only be found in the rain forest.
- The Amazon rain forest will become dry desert if the trees are cut down!

The soil on the ground of a rain forest does not contain many nutrients. They remain in the trees and plants. So when these are cut down, crops do not grow well and the soil erodes and dries out!

Who is destroying the rain forest?

- Big ranchers. They clear huge areas of the forests to feed cattle and sell the meat to hamburger companies.
- Rich logging companies. They cut down thousands of trees. They sell the wood pulp to be made into paper to feed the world with newspapers, magazines and paper products. They sell the wood to make cheap furniture.
- Big multionational companies. They buy huge areas of land to pump oil.

A lot of these activities are illegal. Most of the rain forest is public land. The big companies do not have the right to exploit it.

There are many poor people living in or near the rain forest.They should be allowed to use a small part of the land to grow food for their families. But the big companies chase them away.

WE DEMAND STRICT LAWS TO PROTECT THE RAIN FOREST AND THE LOCAL INHABITANTS!
THE WORLD NEEDS RAIN FORESTS FOR ITS SURVIVAL!
STOP THE DAMAGE NOW BEFORE IT IS TOO LATE! *(345 words)*

Fragen

1. Welchen Beitrag zur Bekämpfung von Umweltverschmutzung leisten die Pflanzen der Amazonas-Regenwälder? (2 Punkte)
2. Warum sind die Pflanzen in den Regenwäldern wichtig für die Medizin? (2 Punkte)
3. Was könnte entstehen, wenn die Bäume der Regenwälder gefällt werden? (1 Punkt)
4. Wer zerstört die Regenwälder (2 Gruppen)? (1 Punkt)

5. Welche Verbindung gibt es zwischen der Herstellung von Hamburgern und der Zerstörung der Regenwälder? (2 Punkte)
6. Wem gehören die Regenwälder? (1 Punkt)
7. Was machen die Großkonzerne mit den Menschen, die in den Regenwäldern wohnen? (1 Punkt)
8. Was verlangen die Autoren des Flugblatts? (2 Fakten) (2 Punkte)

2 *Translate the following paragraph into German.* 12 *pts*

As they left the rain forest behind and the roads improved, Tom began to cheer up. He told Alex all about the boat he shared with his brother.
"I thought we'd take her out onto the reef," he said.
"The Great Barrier Reef?" Alex asked excitedly.
"That's the one," Tom smiled.
Alex grinned. He knew all about the Great Barrier Reef, of course. He'd learnt about it in geography lessons and had always wanted to see the multi-coloured coral for himself. Now he was going to do just that.
"Is it as wonderful as it looks on film?" he asked.
"Better," Tom answered. "A million times better."

8 The Millau Bridge

When we think of a project to build a new bridge, we generally think of it as a feat of engineering skill rather than the work of an architect. However, the Millau Bridge in southern France was actually the idea of an architect, and its climbing, butterfly-like design and minimalist construction techniques may well change forever the way we think about engineering.

The architect was Sir Norman Foster, who is probably best known for his reconstruction of Berlin's Reichstag, and he had the help of one of France's oldest and most respected builders, the Eiffage construction group, who also built the Eiffel Tower. It took Foster and Eiffage over 10 years to plan and build the Millau Bridge, and the result, opened in December of 2004, is one of the longest bridges of its type, and the single tallest road bridge in the world.

The plan was to link Paris to the Mediterranean by high-speed motorway, but the River Tarn in the Massif Central was a serious problem: the Tarn cuts a deep valley between two high plateaus, and traffic had to go down one side of the valley and up the other in order to get across. This caused colossal traffic jams, especially in the summer months, and the effect on the local villages and the environment was less than ideal.

When Foster and Eiffage studied the issue, they realized that simply putting a new bridge over the Tarn would not solve even half the problem: the traffic would still have to cross through the valley, and the construction itself would only worsen the pollution and general chaos in the area. So their solution was this: Why not build a bridge linking the two high plateaus, nearly 300 metres above the River Tarn? Yes, the bridge would need to be longer, but the total damage to the valley would be much less.

Despite its enormous size, the Millau Bridge has an elegant, almost transparent quality which harmonizes with the surrounding landscape. Perhaps more importantly, it was built with a minimum of materials and without doing damage to the environment. And the drive between Paris and the Mediterranean has been shortened by two hours. Norman Foster once said, "Great architecture should wear its message lightly." Perhaps the same could be said of great engineering. *(383 words)*

A TEXT-BASED TASKS 18 pts

1 *Complete the sentences.* 6 *pts*

1. Bridges are usually designed by ______________ rather than by ______________.
2. The Millau Bridge is part of a plan to ______________.
3. The Bridge holds two world records: ______________.
4. The Millau Bridge has been designed to harmonize with ______________.
5. The construction of the bridge hardly did any harm ______________.

2 *Find the information in the text. Answer the questions in complete sentences.* 6 *pts*

1. Before the Millau Bridge was built, how did traffic cross the River Tarn?

____

2. What happened when the traffic crossed the old bridge over the Tarn?

____

3. In what way has the new bridge brought advantages to people driving from the north to the south of France?

____

3 ***Ask questions***
Norman Forster has a website where you can ask him questions. 6 *pts*
Write ***four*** *questions to ask him. Use at least* ***three*** *different question forms.*

1 ______________

2 ______________

3 ______________

4 ______________

B USE OF LANGUAGE *20 pts*

1

*Choose **three** of the following words and phrases and explain their meaning.* *6 pts*

1. respected (line 12) ____________________
2. to link (line 18) ____________________
3. caused (line 23) ____________________
4. chaos (line 32) ____________________

2

Vocabulary – Grammar
Read the text. Find suitable forms of the words and write them down. *14 pts*

The Reichstag building in Berlin has had a (1.) ____________ history. It was (2.) ____________ for the first parliament of the German Empire and opened in 1894. It was set on fire in 1933. The main suspect was a Dutch communist, Marinus van der Lubbe, but until today nobody knows the (3.) ____________. After the (4.) ____________ of National Socialism, the building was left in (5.) ____________. In 1945 the Soviet (6.) ____________ hung their flags from the roof. For many years the building was unimportant, but the garden in front of it was used for (7.) ____________, meetings and pop concerts.

Sir Norman Foster, a British architect, (8.) ____________ to rebuild the Reichstag. It became the seat of parliament again after the opening (9.) ____________ in April 1999. Some people are (10.) ____________ of the unusual (11.) ____________ of old and new elements – the 100-year-old building with a (12.) ____________, modern glass cupola. But in a (13.) ____________ most Berliners said they (14.) ____________ happy with their "new" parliament building.

1.	colour	5.	ruin	9.	celebrate	13.	question
2.	builder	6.	conquer	10.	criticize	14.	be
3.	true	7.	demonstrate	11.	combine		
4.	fail	8.	choose	12.	beauty		

C CREATIVE WRITING *27 pts*

1 ***What advice would you give?*** *8 pts*
Choose **two** *of the following situations and give advice to your friend. Write about 60 words altogether.*

a) Your friend has to cycle home at night on a busy road.

b) Your friend has been given an expensive mobile telephone for his / her birthday.

c) Your friend wants to find out where to do a canoeing course during the holiday.

2 *Choose task A* ***or*** *B. Write about 120 words altogether.* *19 pts*

A *Write an article about your town or village. Describe two buildings and what you can do there. Say why you like it or why you don't like it.*

B *Write a story which starts like this:*
"Yesterday morning my alarm didn't go off."
... and finishes like this:
"What a stroke of luck that I got up late that day!"

D Skills and Techniques *25 pts*

1 *Mediation* *13 pts*

Unten stehend findest du einen Text zum Thema „Brücken auf den Euro-Geldscheinen“. Beantworte die Fragen auf Deutsch.

Bridges on the euro banknotes

Have you ever looked closely at a euro banknote? The front and the back?

Are there famous faces from European history or famous monuments in Europe? The answer is 'no'. On the front of each euro banknote is a picture of a window or a gateway, and on the back of each note is a … bridge! There are seven denominations of banknotes (5, 10, 20, 50, 100, 200 and 500 euros) and each one has a different bridge. But these aren't real bridges which exist somewhere in Europe. They are invented bridges – to symbolize the link between people and countries. So how did a bridge get onto the euro banknotes and who designed it?

In February 1996, six years before the launch of the euro, a competition was held to find the best design for the euro banknote. Forty-four designs were proposed and they were judged by a jury of fourteen experts. The winning design was chosen in December 1996. It was by an artist called Robert Kalina, a banknote designer at the Austrian National Bank. He proposed seven bridges representing seven periods of European history – from Roman times up to the present day. A Roman viaduct is represented on the smallest banknote of 5 euros, and you can follow the historical evolution of architecture through consecutive banknotes right up to a very modern bridge on the 500 euro note. On the front of the note there is a window or a gateway designed in the same style, symbolizing communication between the member countries. Why didn't Robert Kalina draw bridges that already existed? Simply because certain banknotes would be associated with specific countries and that, of course, would go against the spirit of the European Union!

(285 words)

Fragen

1. Welche Darstellungen findet man auf der Vorder- und Rückseite der Euro-Noten? (2 Punkte)
2. Wie wurden die Entwürfe zur Gestaltung der Banknoten ausgewählt? (2 Fakten) (2 Punkte)
3. Was war Robert Kalina von Beruf? (1 Punkt)
4. Was stellen die sieben Brücken dar? (2 Punkte)
5. Was ist a) auf dem 5-Euro-Schein und b) auf dem 500-Euro-Schein abgebildet? (2 Punkte)
6. Was stellen die Fenster bzw. Portale dar? (2 Punkte)
7. Warum hat Robert Kalina nicht reale Brücken gezeichnet? (2 Punkte)

2 *Translate the following paragraph into German.* **12** *pts*

The architect was Sir Norman Foster, who is probably best known for his reconstruction of the Reichstag, and he had the help of one of France's oldest and most respected building companies, which also built the Eiffel Tower. It took over 10 years to plan and build the Millau Bridge, and the result, opened in December of 2004, is one of the longest bridges of its type, and the single tallest road bridge in the world. The plan was to link Paris to the Mediterranean by high-speed motorway, but the River Tarn was a serious problem.